THE ART OF SACRED SMOKE

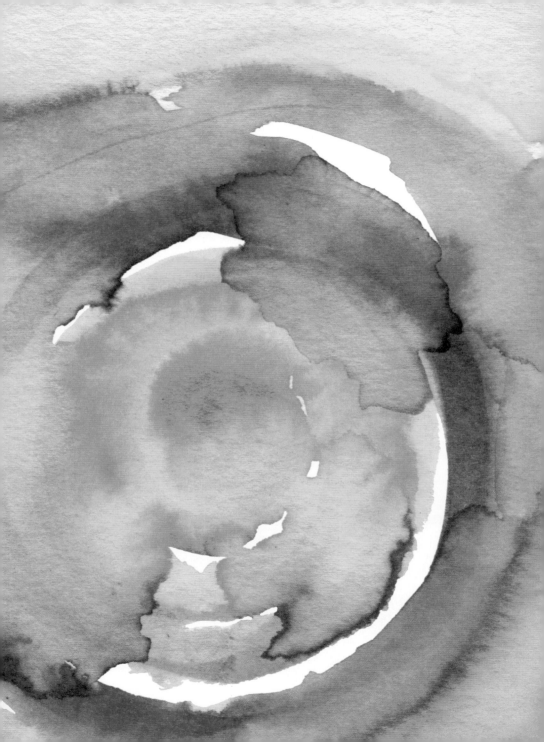

THE ART OF SACRED SMOKE

ENERGY-BALANCING RITUALS TO CLEANSE, PROTECT, AND EMPOWER

NEELOU MALEKPOUR

A TARCHERPERIGEE BOOK

For my grandmothers, my ancestors,

and every teacher who has helped me become

the woman I am today. I am filled with gratitude

for your eternal guidance. I remain present,

ever listening with open eyes, open ears,

and an open heart.

If we go far enough back in time, all of our ancestors under-stood our interconnectedness with the world. It was as basic as breathing. Our ancestors had relationships with other animals, with trees, and other plants, with rocks, earth, and waters, and local spirits of the land that they honored. There was a sacred contract between them to never take more than they needed and to give back to the wider community in the form of offerings, prayers, and rituals. Our blood and bones remember this.

—Jenn Campus

CONTENTS

RITUALS

THE ART OF SACRED SMOKE

INITIATION

INTRODUCTION

I remember the first time I learned about energy and how I could shift my emotions and my mood, even if I couldn't control what was happening in my life. One afternoon when I was in elementary school, I came home, swallowing back tears after a schoolyard slight. I dropped my backpack by the dining room table and ran into my bedroom, hurling myself onto the stuffed animals neatly arranged on my bed. In the safety of my room I cried, my favorite doll Toot Farangi ("Strawberry" in Persian) muffling my sobs.

There was a gentle knock on my bedroom door. I ignored it, twirling my fingers in the doll's thick pink yarn-hair, and braced myself for the "you're too sensitive, school isn't so bad, you need to toughen up" lecture my parents delivered to me almost daily.

I was surprised to see my Maman, my maternal grandmother, instead, wearing her signature red lipstick and a mischievous smile. "I made your favorite," she said in Farsi, scooting me over to sit beside me on the bed. She carried a bowl of *faloodeh* in her chubby hands, a dish of fresh grated apples sprinkled with a bit of sugar and a splash of rosewater.

I was a weird kid at ten years old—my bushy unibrow, intense empathy, and cultural dissonance made me an easy target for bullies. But Maman made me feel calm and grounded because I never felt judged in her presence. I threw my arms around her neck, still not used to her presence. She had just arrived from Tehran, where my family was from.

I was born in Seattle, but I spent the majority of my first four years with both of my grandmothers in Tehran. They share the same first name—Behjat, which means *happiness*—and they took care of me while my parents worked. I was their first grandchild and we were inseparable. I have more memories of them than I do of my mom and dad at that age.

At the height of the Islamic revolution in Iran, when people were disappearing daily because of their political beliefs and the airports had been shut down for months, my parents and I left Tehran illegally with human traffickers, via horseback. I later found out my father made this decision not only because he hadn't been paid by the University of Tehran, where he was an engineering professor, for more than six months, but also because he was afraid for my mother's life—she had just been fired from her job at the National Petrochemical Company, where she was an accountant, because of her anti-revolutionary sentiment. Every day when she left the house, he worried she might not come back because of her very vocal disapproval of the regime change. She refused to cover her hair and adhere to the restrictive new laws that had been instated. To this day there are mass unmarked graves at Behesht Zahra, the largest cemetery in Iran, which contain the remains of those the government felt were anti-revolutionaries.

I remember saying goodbye to my grandparents and my aunts in the middle of the night. I wasn't able to bring any of my belongings so I took the time to say farewell to my dolls and my bedroom. Everyone was so sad, filled with worry. I didn't really understand what was happening but their good-byes felt different, smiles masking dread. That heaviness lingered in me the way bones ache before even a drop of rain falls from the sky. I had no idea I wouldn't see Maman again for almost six years.

My memories of the trip are sporadic but the fear and loneliness I felt are still palpable.

One night we became trapped in a sudden snowstorm on our way to a safe house in the mountains. Blanketed by the falling snow on the mountainside, we had to huddle together for warmth, listening to the howls of wolves nearby. My mother, who rarely cried, sobbed hysterically, wailing with worry that I was going to freeze to death. I remember wanting to tell her I was okay, but I was too cold to speak.

We traveled at night to remain inconspicuous. During the day, we hid in safe houses along the route to Turkey. Once we made it safely there, we hoped to fly to Spain, where we planned to make contact with the U.S. embassy to seek asylum. I was constantly shushed, so I held my breath, afraid we'd be discovered if I breathed too loudly, terrified that I'd be separated from my parents. After seventeen days of torturous travel, we made it to Spain safely, and several months later, the U.S. embassy in Seville granted us all visas to Los Angeles. I often think about how differently things would have played out for us if we had sought refuge in America today.

The journey from Iran to Turkey to Spain to the United States lasted only a few months, but for a long time afterward, I suffered from debilitating separation anxiety. Even now, there's a part of me that waits for the people I love most in this world to disappear with no warning.

Having Maman near me once again lessened my unease, though. That afternoon I silently ate my *faloodeh* while Maman rubbed my back and told me everything was going to be okay. Better than okay, she promised. When I finished, she took my hand and led me to the kitchen. She carefully removed an egg from the refrigerator.

"Neelou, *joonam*, my love, you are a special little girl and your heart is wide open," she said.

She only ever spoke Farsi (which is synonymous to Persian) to me and sweetly pretended she didn't understand if I tried to answer back in English. "What people say and do can feel really painful when your nature is so pure," she continued. "But you have to be forgiving. Not for the sake of others, but because it's the only way to find peace."

I was about to protest when she winked at me.

"Even towards your parents. They love you more than any- thing else in the world but your essence is different. Respect them. Love them. And quietly ignore the things they say and do that feel unnatural to you, and do this without resistance."

The relief I felt at that moment was indescribable.

"I'm going to teach you a little magic. It always makes me feel better," she said brightly. She took a piece of charcoal and started marking little lines on the egg while naming aloud people we knew. When more than half the egg was covered with black tally lines, she asked me to start naming my friends and teachers.

"Liesel, Mrs. Hammer, Kyle, Jason," I whispered. "Am I do- ing it right?" I wondered if this was going to hurt anyone.

"Mmm hmmm. A little louder, *azizam*, my dear," she in- structed. As if she were reading my mind, Maman said, "You must send love to every single person you name. Pray for their health and happiness. *Khob*? Okay?"

Once I finished naming everyone I could think of, Maman placed a small gold coin on top of the egg, holding the coin with her thumb and the bottom of the egg with her index finger.

"Close your eyes and feel your sadness and frustration and anything else that feels bad."

I could hear her whispering names and prayers when my emotions took over. I felt the warmth of tears on my face, a tightness in my chest. And suddenly the egg broke. Immediately I felt lighter. My grandmother chuckled. "Ah. Isn't that better?"

She wiped my tears and kissed me on my forehead. "We're almost done, *azizam*, just one more thing."

"What just happened?" I asked, bewildered and excited.

"Other people's energy can affect us. The more sensitive you are, the more you're affected. In good ways and harmful ways, too—even the most well-intentioned people who love us can inadvertently cause us grief with their own fears. We have to be vigilant about cleansing and protecting our spaces." She started humming as she walked around the house, opening all the windows and the glass door to the patio.

"What we just did cut any negative entanglements between you and others. We don't have much say over what happens to us in this life. The only thing we have power over is our energy. *Fahmidi?* Make sense?"

Her words brought a sense of déjà vu to me. Maman walked back to the kitchen and removed a jar of *Esfand,* Wild Rue seeds, from the cabinet, and poured a little mound in her palm. She touched me on each shoulder with the hand containing the seeds and circled it over my head. Then she poured the *Esfand* into a metal sieve and placed it over the flames from the stovetop. A column of white smoke slowly rose. It smelled pungent and sweet and familiar. "We used to do this together when you were a baby," she confirmed.

Maman fanned the smoke all around me, even under my arms. The knots in my belly unfurled. In that moment I felt a deep sense of power. I felt connected to my Maman and my ancestors and my lineage in a way I never had before. And to this day, every time I cleanse and protect my space, no matter which plant I use, I feel that same bond. It truly is magical.

My maternal grandparents died suddenly, two weeks apart from each other, when I was studying law in New York City. I was devastated and there wasn't even time for me to travel to their funerals. I stopped enjoying school, my relationship with my boyfriend was chaotic, and I wasn't able to process my grief at all. For months I felt lost and like I had no purpose. Doctors prescribed antianxiety medication to help me cope and I felt like a mess of a human.

One night Maman came to me in my dreams. She didn't speak but I could understand her. She walked into my kitchen and found the *Esfand* hidden in the back of my cabinet. I heard the popping of the seeds and my home was filled once again with that sweet, pungent smell. She was reminding me of the magic of these traditions because I'd forgotten.

I woke up feeling better than I had in months and so I started burning *Esfand* regularly. It helped me connect to Maman as if she were still here. It helped me feel grounded and hopeful. And slowly my spiritual journey began to unfold. First with the book *Many Lives, Many Masters* by Brian L. Weiss, which led me to the mystical study of Kabbalah, and then with a reawakened interest in Eastern philosophy and yoga, in which I received my teacher training certification. This all led me to the path of shamanism and The Power Path, where I have been receiving teachings from expert shamans José and Lena Stevens for a decade now.

As I learned more about plant allies, crystals, tarot, astrology, the unconscious mind, and all things metaphysical, the rituals I practiced transformed and multiplied. And after fifteen years of immersing myself in various cultures and sacred texts, I felt a dissonance between my authentic self and what I was doing professionally. This contrast created a desire to integrate my personal and professional lives and as a result my company SMUDGED was born in 2017. My intention in creating SMUDGED was to help people thrive by supporting each individual's process of healing and unlearning. My hope has always been to unite people and to raise the collective vibration by creating natural products that transform one's energetic frequency from fear to love, whether that is a potent crystal-infused spray or a bundle of sacred herbs.

For the past four years, clients have contacted me for a myriad of issues: insomnia, infertility, anxiety, depression, and so much more. Why me? Who am I to help these people? I'm not a doctor or a psychologist and I do not call myself a guru by any means. But I have taken what I have learned from my ancestral lineage and from my many years of teachings to give people holistic solutions for their troubles. And I have seen this audience grow astronomically as people look for alternatives to Western medicine—one way or another, many of us have realized that a quick prescription for a pill is not always the answer.

My intention in writing *The Art of Sacred Smoke* is to provide each reader with the tools they need to cleanse, protect, and empower themselves through the use of natural ingredients and simple rituals—just like the one my Maman taught me. That means you!

My aim is to support you in cultivating your innate power to harness the energy of the elements, so that you may transform your human experience. Congratulations on taking the first step on this journey. Now, let's begin. Always remember to trust your intuition. Cultivate your inner knowing, take what works for you, and leave the rest behind.

CHAPTER 1

WHAT IS THE ART
OF SACRED SMOKE?

THE EVIL EYE

In my heritage, the art of sacred smoke begins with the notion of the evil eye and the simple truth about energy. Energy is real. I say this all the time. It may seem obvious, but I want to clarify what that means to me, and in this book, because it has everything to do with the evil eye—which in my culture, and much of the Middle East, is the notion of someone creating harm in your space with their thoughts or words, either with malicious intent or subconsciously. Sacred smoke rituals are important in setting clear boundaries and protecting against the evil eye, a notion under different names that spans a myriad of cultures and people.

About a decade ago, I participated in a plant medicine ceremony led by a prominent shaman and metaphysical author, the first of several. While he was opening the circle, he shared a lesson that permanently shifted my perspective. Here it is: *There are no secrets*. It may seem that there is much that we don't know about the world, about others and vice versa, but if we get quiet and centered, we have the ability to access the truth about any and everything.

Since then, I've honed my ability to receive information from people and situations regardless of their façade, and you can, too. We've all been there: you walk into your friends' home for a dinner party, and it's clear that the couple has just had a terrible fight. Despite their smiling faces and pleasant welcomes, something is off. You feel uncomfortable. Energy is real; it's where the saying *You can cut the tension with a knife* comes from. If I'm scrolling my Instagram feed, checking out the handles of who has looked at our stories, sometimes I feel a little tap in my solar plexus (and sometimes it can feel like a punch). I've come to realize that the person whose name elicits that tapping feeling has been triggered by me in some way, generally without any intention on my part.

We are naturally drawn to authenticity. Some people are magnetic because of their genuine nature—there is little disparity between their internal and external persona, and we can *feel* it. On the flip side, if we are not mindful of what we are projecting out into the world and specifically toward other people, we can cause harm. How affected we are by others' bad juju depends on our own spiritual mastery. I know some people who are never influenced by others' opinions, words, thoughts, or nature. For most of us, though, especially sensitive folks, empaths, healers, and the like, there are many shades of gray at play. And if we aren't in control of our own energy, we can curse each other without realizing it. We compliment a friend on how beautiful they look, but are simultaneously feeling jealous, or a desire to possess something of theirs, and that can affect our friend negatively.

That's why energetic cleansing is so important, and why employing sacred smoke rituals and other esoteric protective measures is critical. It's like personal hygiene. The same way we wash our hands to prevent disease, or dust and clean our homes, it's essential to cleanse the energetic body. Consider the scientific theory of cause and effect: you bounce a ball against a wall and it's going to come right back, in exactly the same way. You better believe that the negativity you put out is going to bounce back to you in time. This is also the root of Karma. Jealousy, competitiveness, speaking about other people, toxicity, crosstalk, complaining, judging—the less you do, the better you will feel in this world. None of this is easy, but it's a worthy goal. (It's important to note that becoming obsessive about the evil eye is just as harmful as not paying any mind. It's about cultivating balance and self-care, not about becoming superstitious. Constantly worrying about who might be throwing shade your way, or how you might be triggering people, will just fuel that negative juju.)

I invite you to stay out of judgment—of others and especially of yourself. To cultivate a lens of love and compassion. You can do all of the rituals and chant all of the mantras, but if you are still gossiping, wishing negativity on others, spending a lot of time in judgment and envy, if you live by *an eye for an eye*, your actions will negate the blessings you are calling into your life. Again, this is simple cause and effect, not punishment. The Universe always matches what you are putting out, so when you raise your vibration through rituals and then dull it with hostility, your life will come to an energetic standstill and you will be unable to reap the benefits you desire and deserve. Perfection is not necessary but be cognizant of the fact that you cannot live a life of freedom and fun and functionality while spreading the opposite in your actions.

Try to take things lightly. Making a big deal when life doesn't go your way is only going to encourage bad vibes. We are imperfect by nature, so no one is exempt from making mistakes. Awareness and mindfulness are the goals.

A HISTORY OF SACRED SMOKE

The act of using smoke from herbs and flowers to cleanse and purify a person or a space, or in sacred ceremonies, exists in all cultures, spanning all time. While the herbs used and the methods employed vary depending on region or spiritual practice, these ancient rituals are mystical and evocative, unifying all of humanity with the transformative element of Fire. Sacred smoke has the power to magnify the voice of our intuition and to bless everything it touches. It contains the power to deflect and alchemize unwanted energy.

Many of us have been experiencing a desire to shift away from modern Western culture to reclaim our true nature and connect with the essence of our ancestors. These ancient practices evoke a remembering of sorts, allowing us to reconnect to our real selves, who we actually are.

In some cultures, herbs are tied in a bundle, or braided. In others, branches or pinches of herbs are placed directly on an indoor or outdoor fire. Some use a piece of charcoal in a lined, fireproof container and sprinkle their herbs on top, and others use special-made burners. I love using a sieve directly over my stove, the way the matriarchs of my family taught me it—there are many ways to experiment with until you find *your* way.

For me, the most important aspect of burning sacred smoke is a sense of ritual that brings me back to myself, and thereby my emotions, through repetition. It's about taking responsibility for my vibration and how I am showing up in the world, no matter what is happening outside of my control. Spreading this knowledge is my own personal form of activism. My aim is to share my ancestral knowledge to support others in maintaining healthy boundaries and combating the chaotic nature of humanity, so that together we can elevate our collective consciousness.

DEMYSTIFYING MAGIC

When I speak of magic, I am not talking about illusion, or a manipulation of the senses, or unnatural powers. I'm not talking about the wizarding world of Harry Potter, bending spoons, David Blaine, or sleight of hand. I'm speaking of being at one with the natural order of the Universe. Of being in such alignment with our authentic selves that life unfolds with divine grace and flow. This is the epitome of supernatural. In fact, magic is the essence of existence; magic is a state of Universal flow. Magic occurs when we use energy with conscious intent and awareness to attain a better understanding of the world and to harmonize with it.

Magic is a state of being, gratitude personified. It's embracing the beauty that is all around us. It's fine-tuning our senses and intuition. Timing ourselves to the rhythms of the planets, stars, Sun, Moon, and seasons. When we become attuned to nature and the Universe, reality shifts from struggle to flow and life takes on an ethereal quality that feels, well, magical.

In a practical sense, magic can help us live a life of purpose and meaning, while having so much fun along the way. Magic can help us overcome grief, dissipate unresolved childhood issues, unravel patterns in relationships, mend intimacy and commitment issues, and transform our state of receptivity to invite prosperity and abundance. Magic creates space for curiosity. It allows us to be inspired and inspiring. And it can give us the permission we need to be more vulnerable, openhearted, and connected versions of ourselves—making us better parents, teachers, healers, friends, daughters, sons, siblings, and citizens of the world.

UP-LEVELING YOUR FREQUENCY

Imagine being on a road trip. The radio is playing Beethoven but you really want to listen to The Weeknd. What do you do? Change the station, right? This is how our lives work as well. If you're not enjoying your current reality, it's time to change your frequency.

Think of human beings as antennas. We live from the frequency we are tuned in to. Our proverbial radio station is determined by a lot of things: past experiences, habits and choices, what we choose to put into our bodies, how much sleep we're getting, how much we move, the amount and quality of the water we drink, the energies of the people we interact with the most, the media and social media we consume, and the state of our minds—especially our subconscious minds, which are mainly composed of childhood experiences. There is so much that goes into what our lives look like at this present moment, and it's all malleable.

Take some time to consider the various areas of your life and then rate each from 1 to 10, 10 being *amazing*—you are thriving, so no change is necessary; 1 being *dysfunctional*—you are completely out of whack and transformation is needed; 5 being just *fine*—you're not exactly flourishing, but there's also no pain about this particular sphere. It just is.

Be brutally honest, or the changes your soul is craving will elude you. Consider: What are you most longing to transform? Is there a category (or five) that doesn't feel in alignment with your best and highest good? Or where you feel stuck? If so, it's time to change your frequency. It's first necessary to figure out your starting point. This chart will help you decide what to focus on—consider it your current coordinates. In the same way you need to know where you *are* to figure out the best route to your destination, this is the beginning of your journey.

I'm sharing the rituals in this book as a lifelong practice, so that you can change your frequency as needed and start living life from a different "radio station" whenever you are called to. Your life will transform, slowly at first and then quickly when you become cognizant and in control of the vibration you are emitting.

I suggest bookmarking this page and coming back to it each quarter, preferably on the Full Moon. (It is also available to print out from my website, at www.smudged.co.) Allow these questions to support you in creating a road map by contemplating the different areas of your life and considering what needs a little love and reorganization. It might behoove you to connect with a small group of like-minded people and do this together with intentions and goals to keep one another accountable in moving things forward. There is great power in this practice. And great power in sharing your journey with others who can hold space for your process.

HEALTH

Think back on the past couple of weeks. How do you feel? Are you energetic? Sluggish? Do you have lots of little aches and pains? Are you tired or do you feel rested? Are you experiencing sleep issues? How is your digestion? Are you restless or do you feel calm? Are you generally feeling strong or a bit fragile? How is your mind? Do you feel connected? Are you experiencing allergies? Are you having autoimmune flare-ups? How is your overall health?

1 · 2 · 3 · 4 · 5 · 6 · 7 · 8 · 9 · 10

CAREER

How do you feel about your job? Do you have a sense of purpose? Are you excited to go to work or do you get the Sunday scaries? Do you feel challenged? Are you working to live or living to work? Do you feel good about your career or does it feel like a waste of time? Do you feel taken advantage of or appreciated? If money were no object, would you still be doing the work you are currently doing?

1 · 2 · 3 · 4 · 5 · 6 · 7 · 8 · 9 · 10

FINANCES

Is money a source of angst for you? Do you feel like you are earning enough? Are you living with a surplus or a deficit? Are there any specific belief systems around money that might not serve you? Are you living within your means or do you have debt that it's hard to imagine digging yourself out of? Does looking at your bank account stress you out or do you enjoy managing your money? How do you feel about your finances?

1 · 2 · 3 · 4 · 5 · 6 · 7 · 8 · 9 · 10

RELATIONSHIPS

Are you in a healthy relationship or a toxic one? Are you and your partner individuals who have come together or are you unhealthily codependent? Or maybe you long for a partner and feel hopeless about finding one? Do you feel you are seemingly very different from one another? Do you feel taken advantage of or appreciated?

1 · 2 · 3 · 4 · 5 · 6 · 7 · 8 · 9 · 10

BODY IMAGE

When you pass a mirror and catch a glance, what's your inner dialogue? How do you feel about your appearance? Do you really love yourself? Do you feel any shame pertaining to your physical appearance or body in any way? How appreciative do you feel with regard to your physicality? What would you change about yourself and why? Are you able to accept compliments about your appearance with grace or do you deflect them?

1 · 2 · 3 · 4 · 5 · 6 · 7 · 8 · 9 · 10

ENVIRONMENT

How organized is your space? Are you a minimalist or do you have a lot of clutter? Is there a fear of lack you struggle with when attempting to get things organized? When was the last time you did a thorough cleaning? I'm talking drawers, closets, garage, storage, nooks and crannies. How does your space make you feel? Do you feel good in your environment or does it need attention and care? Does your home feel like a sanctuary?

1 · 2 · 3 · 4 · 5 · 6 · 7 · 8 · 9 · 10

CHAPTER 2

EMBRACE THE *JADOOGAR* WITHIN

JADOO

Despite claims to the contrary, the world's oldest profession is probably *witch*. Witchcraft has always existed. A witch is a healer, who like the raven is able to traverse between this realm and others. In the Anglo-Saxon tradition, the etymology for individuals who were herbalists, healers, shamans, magical practitioners, and even priestesses was *wicce* (pronounced *wich*). In the Persian and Indian languages, we use the word *jadoo* (pronounced *jah-doo* in Farsi) for "magic." A *jadoogar* is a medicine woman or man, sorcerer, wizard, or witch. If you're helping heal people, in whatever way, and especially if you have been drawn to this book, in my humble opinion you're already a *jadoogar*. If that freaks you out, you don't need to take on any labels that don't feel right. But to those who feel called, may you adopt this title with confidence and pride. Sisters (and siblings of all genders), may we band together in support of one another and never let anyone dull our light.

Unfortunately, there *still* exists a negative connotation to both *jadoogar* and "witch," with many associating them with insults of the worst kind. In fact, there are some very well-meaning people who are afraid of the work I do because I refer to myself as a green witch, but why? This isn't a purely academic question, but one of life and death. The Colonial American and Early Modern European witch hunts began around 1450 and spanned three hundred years, resulting in an estimated forty thousand executions, mostly of women. There is *still* anti-witchcraft legislation on the books in Cameroon and Saudi Arabia. It's taken almost six hundred years for witchcraft's reputation to improve, with *jadoogar* slowly reclaiming its magical connotation. My hope is that we seize this moment to come together and lessen the hold of fear over our consciousness, instead inviting in curiosity about the cyclical rhythm of nature that will cultivate our own innate knowing.

I am hopeful that we are heading toward a cultural renaissance where humanity recognizes the likeness in all of us, with similarities in genetics and metaphysics and ancestry illuminating the fact that our perceived differences are shallow. An authentic shift from fear, judgment, persecution, and condemnation will ensue, giving birth to a kinder, more empathetic version of humanity that is effortlessly in alignment with nature.

THE POWER OF RITUAL

I created my company, SMUDGED, to bring sacredness to the mundane. The act of ritual transforms everyday life. And as we have all felt, there is quite a bit of darkness in this world, and the pandemic has created even more disconnection and isolation between us. But it's our choice to retreat to the darkness. By reclaiming our power, we can connect to light and beauty instead because our true essence is divine.

Many esoteric teachings say that we are spiritual beings having a human experience. This body we are living in seems real, as does everything we see around us—but what if reality as we know it is an illusion? If you've seen the film *Inception*, consider how real those dreams were to the dreamers, and imagine for one moment the chance that this life is not as it appears and that our soul is somewhere else—a safe haven, a realm where there is no pain, no division, and no sadness, just love. I know how abstract this sounds, but I also know it to be true. And while I'm not asking you to accept this notion, or even understand it, if you can open up to the *possibility*, that's enough to open yourself up to opportunities you never imagined. Belief or hope in possibility is necessary to reap the benefits of the rituals presented in this book. If your rational mind is struggling, can you muster a one percent belief?

So, what is ritual? I define it simply as a series of mindful actions supported with intention. Ritual can build a bridge between our worldly selves and our otherworldly selves. Coupled with a commitment to a daily practice, rituals serve as a dynamic method to reclaim our power when we're feeling powerless for any reason. So, if you are feeling out of control, lost, confused, hopeless, helpless, or weak in any way, you can restore your equilibrium through ritual. And if you're already feeling good, ritual will allow you to connect to the idea of Universal oneness. Sprinkle in the element of Fire, and the transformations will unfold exponentially.

If you're reading this, it's a sign, a message that you are already powerful beyond measure. That you can choose a new path, perhaps one that is foreign and you feel completely unprepared for. Nothing in your present reality defines your future. *At all*. Consider each shattered dream a stepping-stone. If you think it's too late, check yourself because there's no such thing. That's just a construct. If you think your desires are out of reach, question that thought. Who says? F them. While acknowledging and respecting the destruction it has left in its wake, one of the lessons that COVID-19 taught us is that literally anything is possible. Use these rituals to shape-shift. To transform. To reclaim your sense of self. The more you invite ritual into your life, the more you will remember who *you* are. And you will know with every fiber of your being that anything you dream can be. You are infinitely powerful and the Universe has your back.

Before we go further, let's address *toxic positivity*, or the notion that we should shun our negative emotions and solely focus on the glass-half-full aspects of life. It's a diversionary tactic—a way to suppress emotions and gaslight others by denying their lived experiences. Well-meaning or shut-down people can perpetuate it unintentionally; sometimes it's straight-up manipulation. Ignoring difficulty and suffering will harm us just as much as fixating on it, because pain demands to be felt. We must be willing to look at the full spectrum of our true feelings. If we can create space to become curious about our less desirable emotions and move toward them instead of pushing them away, we can bear witness to the wisdom our experiences are bestowing upon us. We can use the shadows as a catalyst for change. That said, attempting to effect change from a place of pessimism is akin to trying to jump a wall with heavy weights around your ankles. The move is to feel your feelings and then shift your focus as quickly as possible. Keep the energy moving. For myself, I know that if I indulge in negativity—tuning into sensational news, or watching people argue about politics on social media—it wipes me out for days.

This goes for others as well. I suggest you steer clear of giving advice when not specifically asked and be mindful of judging others. We can never truly know what another is going through, and there simply isn't enough grace and kindness in our basic interactions right now. Every human can benefit greatly from a friend who can serve as a sounding board, someone who is willing to just listen. With that said, it is important to maintain strong boundaries when it comes to what emotions we allow others to introduce into our space, too.

Your healthy boundaries will upset toxic people, who may be offended by you if you are unwilling to validate a dialogue focusing on negative feelings, bad news, political drama, gossip, or fill in the blank. They may even call your constructive choice to raise your vibration by limiting your exposure to counterproductive behaviors toxic positivity. Do not get it twisted, those people are mistaken. If you take a peek into the lives of those you find most inspirational, balanced and successful, they're probably counting their blessings, and focusing on gratitude for what's working, more than indulging in what's wrong.

It is more important than ever to exercise our attitudinal muscles. In the same way that a couple of months of sedentary living will atrophy muscles that were once well-defined, if we do not tone our mental outlook, we cannot thrive. When we are caught in a pattern of negativity, despair, or worry, there is little room for power or for magic.

Imagine a dark room, so dark you can't even see your hand in front of your face. The simple act of lighting the smallest flame drives the darkness away. This is the potential of this book, and if you walk away from reading it with just one takeaway, I hope it is a desire to step consciously into your power through the act of intentional ritual.

INTUITION AND DEVELOPING YOUR SENSES

Intuition is how you interpret and understand information processed by the senses without involving your intellect. It's the ability to comprehend something viscerally. Intuition is a nuanced power. In the same way that we have varying learning styles (auditory, linguistic, kinesthetic) and multiple love languages (service, time, gifts), hearing the voice of your intuition can look different for each of us. Some get a gut feeling connected to the solar plexus, while others see visual imagery or receive the information from the top of their head, which is connected to the crown chakra.

It's helpful to be able to hear the voice of your intuition, because if you are tuned in and are able to hear what is being communicated, it can feel like having a superpower. If you're detached, it can be elusive, even nonexistent. On the other side of this spectrum are the people who are born with a robust intuition that can feel overwhelming. In fact, one of the most common questions I get through SMUDGED is how to tap into one's intuition.

My sixth sense, as many call it, has been on fleek since the 1980s and it's been a wild journey! As a kid, whenever either of my parents were stressed, which they often were (a normal state of being for two people who endured a violent revolution in their home country before fleeing to a foreign land with a toddler, leaving all of their family and friends and belongings behind, and then having to figure out life from scratch), I was an anxious ball of nerves. Little Neelou suffered a lot from tummy aches, nausea, a sensation of having knots in my belly, and a difficult time sleeping, especially alone, until I was a teenager.

The smallest imbalance would send me reeling. And the fact that my parents never shared any of their troubles with me— trying to pretend like life was just peachy as most good parents do, sheltering kids from problems beyond their age—didn't help because my imagination was out of control. My brain would take the slightest twinge from my intuition and create the most dramatic story possible. I felt like a can of soda that had been dropped on the floor.

These days, I wake up just a minute before an earthquake hits. I have dreams, good and bad, that come to pass. When something catastrophic is going to happen on a world scale, I'm practically sick with generalized worry the week before. I sometimes know a friend is pregnant even before they do. If something's the matter with someone close to me, it's literally like that person is tapping me on the shoulder, trying to get my attention. And good luck to anyone trying to keep a secret, whether it has anything to do with me or not. Even a fun surprise I experience as being lied to. It's an uncomfortable feeling. But the more time I spend relating to this sense, the more I am able to decipher its nuances. I've learned never to ignore a clear *no*, whether or not it makes rational sense, because it's always right.

So everyone wants to know about intuition and how to tap into it. A lot of the practices in this book are about receptivity, or immersing yourself in the receptive state. *Allowing*, instead of ignoring, repelling, or tuning in the mind—as most people are taught to do when making decisions—is the first step. Spending as much time as you can in the receptive mode will give voice to your intuitive abilities.

PRACTICE: AWAKEN YOUR INTUITION

The voice of the mind and ego are loud, and intuition is more like a whisper—a gentle knowing. I've never met a person without an intuition, but if hearing that voice does not come naturally, that's not unusual. It's a latent tool waiting for you to access it. The key is to practice so you can recognize what it feels like and then exercise it so it becomes easier to hear. Like with most things in life, consistency is fundamental. Try this exercise daily for a month to get going.

Before you go to sleep and when you wake up in the morning, say the following intention aloud or quietly to yourself—you can put it on a Post-it note or even write it with lipstick or a dry erase marker on a mirror you see frequently: *I welcome the voice of my intuition. My inner vision is strengthening every day. I am intuitive. I am knowing. Show me how to trust my inner guidance.*

Carve out a few minutes during your day to sit quietly with your eyes closed. Take some deep breaths, allowing your consciousness and your body to settle. Repeat your affirmation. Again, take some deep breaths, allowing your consciousness and your body to settle. Sit and simply be mindful. Is your body giving you any messages? Do you feel any sensations of lightness or heaviness? There is no need for effort here. Relax your face and shoulders and release any tension you are holding on to in any other parts of your body.

Now think about something in your life you would like more insight into. Focus on it from a place of neutrality, removing emotion. You can do this! Again, take deep breaths and pay attention to the thoughts that emerge. Stay in this space a bit longer than what feels comfortable—usually the intuitive messages come forth once the ego has had its say.

Open your eyes and immediately write down all that came to you. Repeat this practice daily. With time, you will see the messages coming from your *sixth sense* have a different feeling than those presented by the mind, and your intuition will begin to strengthen and become more noticeable. While you may feel frustrated at first, keep at it and the changes will transpire!

SELF-CARE IS THE CRUX OF MAGICAL BEINGS

If you're tired, stressed out, and run down, it's going to be difficult to raise your vibration enough to reap the benefits of any magical practices. In the same way you probably wouldn't be able to run a marathon without the proper fuel and training, if our bodies are not in optimal condition, we become tethered to the realm of time and space and stop the flow available to us in any given moment. We need self-care because it's impossible to be of any use to the world when we are depleted and drained.

Self-care will look different for each person depending on the day and current state of things. Here are the basics in no particular order:

* Drink water—plenty of it. There is a magic to being properly hydrated that I can't explain. It's not just about physical health. Water serves as a lubricant in all areas of life. When my clients drink enough water, money flows more naturally, their bodies deflect lower energetic vibrations

with greater ease, and any toxins they're carrying are flushed out. With proper hydration, our physical vessel becomes a conduit for Universal energy. Make sure you drink clean, uncontaminated water that has never been distilled and skip the single-use plastic bottles.

* Get enough sleep. Rest is not optional if you want to call in your best and highest good.

* Unplug. The first time I attended a Vipassana meditation retreat—which has an atmosphere that's the opposite of a cushy spa—it also was a necessary tech detox. In the middle of nowhere, for ten days, you have no access to your phone or electronics, and can't journal, read, or exercise; are not allowed to speak or even communicate nonverbally; you're assigned chores like cleaning the shared toilets; and you wake up before dawn every day to begin your meditation practice. It was life changing and ego crushing, and highlighted the importance of disconnecting from technology to truly connect to myself. Now I usually take every Sunday off from all electronics (my goal is to take two consecutive days off but that has not happened yet). Taking this break from the phone, social networks, TV, and my computer has been the most loving, kind, soothing thing I have done for myself in recent years. On weeks that I skip my tech cleanse, I feel *off*. If you can't commit to one full day, that's okay; begin somewhere. Are

you willing to put your phone on airplane mode before you sleep and keep it that way until you've done all of your morning rituals? Can you skip your intake of news or reality TV one night a week? Find something that feels outside of your comfort zone but that you will be able to commit to and do it.

* Eat clean. I eat plant-based; I almost never drink alcohol—heck, I don't even take Advil—but I know that's extreme for most people, and I'm not saying any of that should be your goal. Instead, remember: *you are what you eat.* It's a cliché because it's true. What we consume is transformed into energy that our body and brain use to function. So how can you eat better, on a more consistent basis? I always recommend that my clients first consider their consumption of animal products. Are you able to reduce your intake just a little? If you are eating animals grown with antibiotics and living in subpar conditions, in fear and despair, that's the energy you are introducing into your system, and even the most responsible animal farming is deteriorating the Earth's atmosphere at a faster rate than any other pollutant. Eat lots of fresh fruit and veggies, fewer processed foods, and less processed sugar. Choose organic as often as possible, and if you can't, wash your produce well with a natural cleanser like vinegar or salt water. When our bodies are balanced and healthy, rituals and

spiritual work go so much faster, and life unfolds with grace and flow.

* Movement. Exercise is important for the same reasons that healthful food is. Living an active life keeps you healthy and helps release toxins. Fewer toxins means less resistance to multidimensional practices. You don't need to be a tri-athlete, just move in a way that feels good for your body, whether that's solo dance parties, yoga, walks, running, or playing soccer. Do it regularly, at least a few times a week, to keep your vessel vibrant.

* Environment. This includes everything from literal clutter to whom you spend the most time with. Marie Kondo speaks the truth: tidying up your physical space also carries a mystical component. If disorder is made orderly with intention, it will simultaneously organize your mind and discharge long-held belief systems that no longer serve you. Take an inventory of your life—what and whom does your environment comprise? Rid it of excess, clutter, and toxins. Also remove gossip, comparison, jealousy, and friends who don't bring out the best in you, naysay your dreams, or dull your vibration. None of this is easy, but if you rid your life of the burdens that keep you tethered to dysfunction, you can sit back and watch the beauty that grows in its place.

* Boundaries. The B word. I could dedicate an entire book to this topic but suffice it to say healthy boundaries equal functional relationships. The nature of our boundaries ensures how others treat us. Good boundaries provide a secure container for mutually respectful and aligned relationships. Ultimately, having healthy boundaries is a reflection of our own self-worth and self-esteem.

* Nature. Spending time in nature is a necessary act of self-care, which we'll go into in depth in chapter three.

* Ritual. Observing a random Sunday with a candle ritual and bath, or celebrating the Full Moon by gathering ocean water to cleanse your crystals, or making the time for any of the practices in this book, is an act of self-care. Every time you make space for a ritual, you are filling your cup.

* Play. Don't be afraid of getting silly. You can do all the rituals and work all the time, and do all the busy, responsible things and make all the money, but what is a life without fun and laughter? Is there even a point? Making time for play brings magic into our lives because the more time we spend in lighter emotions, connecting to joy, happiness, excitement, and fun, the quicker transformations take place. I have been known to get a little carried away with work so if I have a lot of things going on I actually calendar in fun, the same way I would a meeting or an important

call. My alarm clock plays "Into the Groove," so I always wake up dancing. I also have an alarm set for three p.m. every day, when I stop whatever I'm doing for a one-song dance party, usually alone and sometimes with my pup, Palo Santo. It's instant bliss. Try it.

A woman armed with ancestral wisdom is a powerful force. You'll find her powers come from within—she is in tune with her spirit and the magic of the Universe. She trusts, values, and follows her intuition.

—Lori Bregman

CHAPTER 3

MAGIC OF NATURE

ALIGNING WITH NATURE

The quickest way to become attuned to your energetic state is to become harmonized with the frequency of nature. Connecting to the Earth is an essential daily practice. If I were to recommend only one ritual, one practice, that has the most transformative propensities, it would be a daily connection to Mother Earth, or *Pachamama*.

I start every day (and hopefully soon, you will too) by dropping a root into the Earth. Connecting to Pachamama, even figuratively, synchronizes us with our truest selves. (See page 46 for this rooting, or grounding, exercise.) As I write, I'm sitting in the middle of Joshua Tree, California, with nothing but desert and critters for miles in every direction. The Sun is hot. The breeze is blowing, and Palo Santo is resting his chin on my toes—life in the desert is grounding for both of us. He is much calmer, barely barking here, and it's easier for me to write.

My creativity flows when I'm surrounded by nature, or at the very least connecting to it on a daily basis. I was a die-hard city girl for many years, of that breed who deems New York City as the center of the Universe and can't fathom living anywhere else. In fact, I was this person for most of my life. But after I launched SMUDGED, all that glass and concrete that used to feel energizing started to feel stifling. I'd look around craving space but all I could see were buildings. I felt called to move to a city more in tune with the elements, and the Universe led me to Miami Beach, which feels like a *National Geographic* spread in comparison to New York City. Wherever you find yourself, connecting to nature on a regular and consistent basis is necessary in cultivating a state of flow and grace in your life.

Whether you live in a remote area surrounded by the elements or in a concrete jungle, you can make that happen. When I worked on Park Avenue, the second the weather was semibearable, I'd leave my office, walk to the median of grass that divided opposing traffic, and take off my shoes and socks, feeling the grass under my bare feet. Regardless of the strange looks I received, on the days I carved out those fifteen minutes, I felt different—calmer, less anxious, and able to think more clearly.

If this is a part of your life already, good for you! If you are a city dweller, or are simply accustomed to spending most of your time indoors, take some time right now, before reading any further, to get creative and make a list of ways to connect with the Earth on a regular basis. Here are ideas to start you off:

* Wake up with the sunrise. Go outside and do some Sun Salutations, preferably barefoot or without a mat, which will link you directly to Pachamama.
* Plant a garden. If you live in an apartment, plant something on your terrace, or even inside on the windowsill. I have a healthy mint plant flourishing in my kitchen.
* Fill your home with plants—all kinds. Touch their soil daily. Communicate by singing to them, chatting with them, and lovingly cleaning their leaves.
* Hug a tree. Literally. And for longer than it feels comfortable.
* Watch the Full Moon rise. Spend time just gazing at it.
* Get some vitamin D. Bathe in the Sun daily. Depending on your individual melatonin levels, just twenty minutes is great.
* Take a swim in the ocean. Dunk your head beneath the water and let the salt water permeate your being.
* Get fresh flowers for your altar—preferably from a garden or patch of wildflowers (from a spot that you can confirm isn't being overharvested) rather than a store. Choose the

flowers mindfully and feel their vibe. Cultivate gratitude from your heart for their beauty and the energy they bring into your home.

* Shop at your local farmer's market. Get to know your farmers. Can you visit the farm? Are you able to help pick any crops—even just once? If you eat eggs, find a humane farm (not just for the certification but one that doesn't practice culling or beak trimming) and visit the chickens. Feed them, talk to them, and become closer to your food sources.
* Visit hot springs and bathe in the natural spring water.
* Interact with the animals and critters while respecting their space. If you have land—you don't need much—start a beehive, a butterfly garden, or keep it simple and install a bird feeder.

GROUNDING

This simple practice is the most important one in this book. If you were to ignore every other piece of my advice but perform this daily, your life would transform immensely. Every time I work with a client, this is where we begin. I do this exercise every morning and whenever I'm feeling ungrounded in any way. Connecting to the Earth is the fastest way to become fully present and embodied. She is the fabric of our being.

The act of grounding into Pachamama facilitates release, transmutes negativity of any kind, helps with energetic alignment, and brings clarity, focus, and more. Try this exercise every day as the first part of your morning ritual. Her support aids in releasing the negative energy that comes up. You don't need any tools. It is wonderful to be able to be physically connected to the Earth— think shoes off, feet in the grass—but not necessary. Most often I ground sitting at home in front of my altar. I suggest you try both indoors and outside to see the difference.

PERFORM THE RITUAL

Close your eyes and take three deep breaths.

Imagine a golden root growing from your hips, your perineum—your root chakra—down into the ground. Feel it penetrating the layers of the Earth, tunneling deeper and deeper. If you have trouble imagining this, just make it your intention. Let this golden root become stronger as it travels farther down until you reach the center, the molten core of the Earth.

Allow your root to connect to Pachamama's heart, taking a couple of deep breaths to honor this union. Take a moment to cultivate gratitude in your heart for all that she provides for us, and invite her energy to travel up your root and into your body. There's no need to make a huge effort here or push so it feels unnatural.

Scan your body, from the top of your head to your toes,

noticing any thoughts, emotions, and physical ailments that no longer serve you. What thoughts are causing you discomfort? What feelings do you want to shift? Are you holding tension anywhere—your jaw, your neck, or your back? Imagine each thing that is coming up for release as a dark orb moving down your body and out of the root.

Ask Pachamama to transmute everything you are releasing into fuel and love for herself, like fertilizer. Scan your body and mind as many times as you need until there is nothing left for you to release. Once this process feels complete, give gratitude to the Earth and move your attention to the top of your head—your crown chakra.

Imagine a golden, pearly, iridescent funnel ascending toward the sky from the top of your head. Envision this funnel going straight up past the ceiling and the roof (if you're indoors), past any potential clouds or overcast, and connecting you to the Sun. Invite the light and warmth of the Sun into your space, bringing that energy down from the sky and straight into your crown chakra.

It's equally important to know when *not* to ground. This little nugget of knowledge has made many rituals infinitely more effective for me. The Earth is a stabilizing, grounding force. Prayer, meditation, and mantras have a specific frequency we are creating and dialing into, cultivating powerful energy. Grounding into the Earth discharges energy so it can have the opposite effect we want, depending on our goals. Additionally, because the Earth is so grounding, placing a physical boundary like a blanket under the body parts touching the ground while meditating is ideal. The same is true for tools we might use, as the Earth has the power to remove the charge from an object. So, if you're working with a programmed object like a crystal or *mala* (prayer beads), it's best not to place it on the ground. This will ensure the object maintains the frequency you created through your personal process.

EMBRACING THE ENERGY OF THE SEASONS

The four seasons are an integral part of life on this planet. Not only are all things affected by the weather, what is growing around us, and the hours of daylight, but the change in season also plays a big role in human consciousness and mood. When I moved to New York City, I was surprised to realize how hard seasonal depression hit me. By February, with the holiday lights gone and warm weather still a good two to three months away, it felt like one long hangover. The communal drop in serotonin level was palpable. Weather is powerful!

The seasons have symbolic meaning, too, and we can harness the energy of these transitions. I always plan a ceremony to coincide with each equinox and solstice, as they are ideal times to plant seeds of intention. It's not like your intentions won't come to fruition if you perform the same exact ritual at another time of year, but finding the right timing can support the process and allow your dreams to flourish with less effort.

It helps to think of this in relation to gardening. Take tulips, for example. Tulip bulbs require cold weather to bloom properly. In fact, they need at least twelve weeks of cold so they can effectively store nutrients from the soil. If you plant your tulip bulbs in the fall, you can be sure to have a beautiful spring bloom. But if you plant them in April, chances are the soil will be too warm and either they won't bloom at all or if they do, they won't have the same beauty. It's the same with ritual. Here is what you should know about how to harness the specific power of each season:

SPRING

The first day of spring is the Persian New Year and the beginning of the year for not only Iranians. Many cultures have celebrations ranging from late March to mid-April:

* Holi. Known as the Festival of Colors for Hindus, it commemorates the triumph of good over evil.
* Ostara (or Eostra). A celebration of fertility of the Earth that is observed by Wiccans and Pagans.

* Norooz. The Persian and Baha'i new year, which celebrates the return of spring and new life.
* Pesach (or Passover). Within Judaism, this commemorates the Israelites' freedom from slavery, and its spiritual significance is freedom from challenges of the present, from our egos and our inhibitions, from fears, habits, prejudices, and judgments.
* Easter. This Christian celebration is all about rebirth and resurrection, in perfect alignment with the energy of spring.

The energy of rebirth and renewal available during the spring season peaks at the vernal equinox (which changes every year since it's dependent on the lunar calendar). My suggestion to my clients is to recommit to their New Year's resolutions on the first day of spring.

Here are journaling prompts I also recommend. You can use the insight you gain to set an intention of what you would like to birth at this time. Then build a simple ritual around your intention, including some elemental action like planting seeds in a garden.

* What kind of world do you want to live in? Imagine this with your five senses and really delve in.
* What actionable steps can you take to work toward creating this world, beginning with your personal circle?

* What are the limiting beliefs you are carrying that are getting in the way of this dream?
* If you had a genie who could easily remove your limiting beliefs, how would you feel?
* Are you able to connect to those feelings now, in any way? Be creative.

SUMMER

Midsummer, also known as Litha (and many other names, depending on which ancient culture you are consulting), is the longest day and shortest night of the year and steeped in Pagan tradition. It takes place around June 21 but again, varies a bit each year, marking a celebration of light and an anticipation of the slower seasons to come. Since the Sun has reached its peak and nature has completed its cycle of growth, on this day, it's a time to honor your recent wins and successes.

An appropriate ritual would be one of celebration and gratitude. I usually throw a fête on the summer solstice inviting my closest friends to gather in praise—of ourselves and of one another. We rejoice for all that we have achieved in the past year, with flower crowns and champagne or fresh watermelon mocktails. I don't think women celebrate ourselves enough—we are too busy doing. This is the time to stop and admire our triumphs.

Here are several midsummer journaling prompts. You can use the insight you gain to set an intention of what you would like to celebrate. Then build a simple ritual around your bounty and commemorate it in whatever way feels authentic to you.

* What wins have you experienced recently—big and small?
* What have you accomplished this year that makes you feel really proud?
* Bring to mind a pattern you have overcome; name it. How does it feel to be free from its control?
* What is your favorite thing about your life right now?

FALL

Hello, pumpkin *everything*! This is my favorite time of year. Growing up, I thought it was summer I loved most, because I'm a Leo, because no school, because of Sun and pool and fun. But as I've gotten older, I've come to appreciate fall's complexities. There is a profound shift that happens as the leaves change color, elevating their beauty before falling away, and the autumnal equinox makes transformation feel effortless. Unlike the summer solstice, spending this first day of autumn in solitude will facilitate healing and change.

Here are some journaling prompts for autumn. You can use them to gain clarity around that which is coming to the surface to be released, then create a ritual to let go of anything that no longer serves you.

  * What do you believe might be holding you back in your life?
  * What or whom do you need to forgive? Why?
  * In what ways would you feel better if you no longer held on to those resentments? Create a separate answer for each.
  * What is no longer serving you in your life and needs to be released?
  * What would you truly lose, deep down, if you lost what you were most scared of losing?
  * Are you giving your power away to anyone close to you?
  * What habit or pattern of yours is keeping you small?

WINTER

The winter solstice is a big one for my people and we call it Shab-e Yalda. In the northern hemisphere, it's the longest night of the year. It is believed that darkness runs rampant that night, so friends and family come together in protection and celebration because sunrise the following day signals the triumph of Mithra, the god of light, over evil.

I've always loved this night because when I was little we got to stay up late for a big party. Until her recent passing, my paternal grandmother had a celebration at her house each year. Our friends and family gathered together, eating pomegranates, laughing and dancing into the night. Each of us would make a wish and then "randomly" choose a page in a book of poetry by Hafez (a fourteenth-century Persian poet akin to Shakespeare). The poem you selected was the answer to a wish you had made, and the elders would recite it for you. I never understood exactly what they were saying, but everything about the night felt mystical. I still celebrate Shab-e Yalda, even though I no longer live near my family, and since I don't know how to read Hafez, I consult the tarot instead.

Here are some journaling prompts for the winter solstice. Use these questions to connect to your heritage and ancestors, then create a ritual to deepen and strengthen that bond. Remember to mention that only beings of one hundred percent light are welcome into your space.

* What questions do you have about your heritage? Is there anyone in your family you can ask?
* Do you have any relics from your grandparents or great-grandparents?
* What are some of the traditional practices of your people?
* Can you incorporate any of them into your personal rituals?
* What area of the world are your ancestors from? (DNA tests are au courant, and you can get a lot of information that way, but there are privacy concerns to consider first.)

* What would you ask your great-grandmother, or another ancestor, if you could? Write them a letter and invite the answers to come forth through enchanted communication.
* Have you had any past-life recollections that might explain specific rituals or cultures you feel connected to?

My favorite thing about celebrating the seasons through intentional acts of ritual is getting the sense that time is slowing down. I get borderline irate when I see holiday decorations up in September and I refuse to shop at establishments that use them as a marketing ploy. It feels like time is being taken away from me whenever I am plucked from the present and launched months into the future. Relishing the current season, both with regard to the time of year and, in a greater sense, the season of your life, connects us to the present moment—which is the pinnacle of power. Open yourself up to the now, examine what each season is here to teach us, and bond with your heritage. Remember who you are.

HARNESSING THE POWER OF THE SUN, MOON, PLANETS, AND STARS

These astrological insights are just as important as the seasons, and may even have a bigger effect on our lives. The majority of the products we make at SMUDGED are created under auspicious planetary timing, and there are many books out there written by knowledgeable astrologers that can guide you as far as power days and times of each year. Keeping in mind that I am not an astrologer, I am happy to share the basics of timing.

The New Moon represents new beginnings. It's a time to dream and plant seeds and intentions. This is the Moon phase in which I begin larger projects, create my Future Imagined Memories, and set clear intentions for the next time period.

The Crescent Moon brings fresh energy. It's a time to move from *what* to *how*, so you can conceptualize and focus on details. I make any adjustments I feel are necessary to my morning and evening routines during this time so that they support any intentions I've set.

The First Quarter Moon is aligned with taking action and making commitments. There is momentum here in working toward the intentions you set during the New Moon. This is usually my busiest time of the month because it's about staying active and committed to good habits. I always ask myself how I can create maximum output with minimum effort, as this is my personal definition for productivity.

The Gibbous (or Waxing) Moon is about refining and aligning. Question what is working and what is not. It's also a time to be patient with the seeds of desire you've planted. Change doesn't usually happen overnight.

The Full Moon is the peak of the Moon cycle, a heightened time of energy and emotions. Whatever you are feeling or experiencing is intensified during this phase. It's a time of completion, release, and celebration of endings. Cleanse your crystals during this time, and store water from the ocean for future rituals. It's when I make a lot of our limited products, and I always do a personal ritual to harness its power.

The Disseminating (Waning) Moon is about gratitude and acceptance. Take a step back and objectively analyze the facets of your life and existence to see what might be coming up for the next Moon cycle. Consider what to focus on next. This would be a good time to fill out the chart in chapter one.

The Third Quarter Moon has similar energy to the Gibbous Moon but it's a good time to give back and be charitable, to others or oneself. This is an ideal time to change routines and break the habits that don't serve you. I think of this as the "admin" Moon—a time to do the things I've been putting off: cleaning up clutter and wrapping up any loose ends that need to be dealt with. This includes open-ended projects I keep meaning to get to. Make something a priority or shelve it.

The Balsamic Moon is the time to rest and recharge. Self-care is my mantra now. I work less, spend more time in nature, and do a technology cleanse to reset.

The Void Moon is a moment of stillness. I wouldn't recommend launching a new project, planting new seeds, or doing manifestation rituals now. Get some well-deserved rest.

Lunar eclipses happen at least twice a year when the Sun, Moon, and Earth line up. These are intense periods of time and serve as portals to rapid change and growth. Think of a tunnel that allows you to bypass a longer journey toward your aims.

CHAPTER 4

PREPARATION

BEST PRACTICES

The majority of the messages I receive are from people wondering how to use sacred smoke. People are curious about what direction to let the smoke waft in. Whether they should use matches or a lighter. If there is an order to what parts of the house should be cleansed first. Head to toe? Or feet first? Clockwise? Counterclockwise? Should they use an abalone shell? A feather? In my experience, there's only one thing you can do wrong, and that's to not open windows. While this might seem like common sense, the volume of messages I've received with some version of "I just smudged my house and I'm really dizzy, do you know why?" is truly astounding. Me: "Did you open a window?"

When it comes to sacred smoke, the only must is proper ventilation. For two reasons: 1. You can get sick from smoke inhalation; it's straight-up dangerous. 2. Negative energy and matter needs someplace to go. If there's no way out, it's going to stay put. Everything else you have heard about the how-to's of sacred smoke is some version of preference and/or tradition.

Some people use matches only and are offended at the mention of a lighter. Others only walk clockwise. Some cleanse their homes on the Full Moon, and some on the New. Some have specific rituals for the various herbs they use. The reason that most sacred smoke kits (not ours) are sold with shells and feathers (wrapped in plastic, no less) is because the four items are a physical representation of the four elements—the plant is Earth; lighting the herb represents Fire; the abalone shell denotes Water; and the feather, Air. While that's a beautiful notion, and I respect all the traditions of sacred smoke, I don't utilize a feather, nor do I own an abalone shell. I prefer matches, but if I'm outside, a lighter makes much more sense, and I use sacred smoke almost every day, so the timing of the Moon is not essential to my practice. And so on . . .

The fact is, when asked (and a lot of times when not), most people will give you their opinion on how you should do—well, anything, really. The crux of this book, and any spiritual practice, is to cultivate your *own* intuition and home in on listening to what works for *you*, which will probably change day to day or year to year. I suggest starting with the following as a foundation, and then seeing where it takes you. Just start *somewhere* to outsmart overwhelm.

* Always open a window, or make sure there is sufficient ventilation.
* Set a mindful, singular intention. I will keep repeating this, *intention is everything*. Period. In every aspect of life, in burning sacred smoke, and especially when performing a ritual of any kind. Intention is the single most important part of any ritual or act.
* Ground yourself and connect to the Sun (or the Universe) when appropriate. If you are using a mantra, like the Lakshmi mantra, or if you are channeling healing energy, as in the Eye Shakti ritual in chapter seven, you don't want to ground because it would oppose the intelligence of the ritual. (It is, however, good practice to ground yourself at some point each day. I usually do it in the mornings after I've done all my mantras and processes.)
* Open sacred space (see page 69).
* Pay homage to the cultures and teachers who have brought you these practices.
* Give thanks to the plants and tools you are using.
* Connect to your heart, not your ego.
* Practice consistency and throw any notions of perfection in the trash.

* Be mindful and use only the amount you need. Don't burn too much of the plant needlessly; a little goes a long way.
* Do the ritual, whatever it may be.
* Take a moment of silence sending your Namaste energy out into the world.
* Close sacred space (see page 70).
* Go about your day having elevated your frequency and plugged into Universal Intelligence.
* Thank yourself for showing up and making time for radical self-care.

Intention, commitment, and belief are a trifecta of support for your magical invocations. If one of the three is missing, your ritual will be futile.

Let's talk about intention first. Intention is like a lightning bolt of energy paving the path toward where you are hoping to go—not unlike the concept of a magic wand. Not having an intention is like getting in the car and driving with no destination in mind. Or like going to a restaurant and asking the server to order for you. Your dinner will be a surprise you may or may not like. Ya feel me? Intention is the initial layer of support. When you have a clear, singular intention, the Universe begins conspiring on your behalf, moving you into the direction of your dreams. I always include the phrase *for my best and highest good*, no matter what my intention. This way I am making sure that what my human nature desires is not in direct conflict with what might be best for me karmically speaking.

The second pillar is commitment. What happens when we are noncommittal about anything is that our indecision sends out competing frequencies of desire into the Universe. Let's say you're dating someone more than casually but you're not yet exclusive. Emotionally you're one foot in, one eye looking out for something better, or just scared to dive in completely. Your relationship will not work out. It can't. You will end up going your separate ways unless you are willing to commit fully. This isn't even about what you're willing to share with another person; it's an internal decision. It's about energy. You must commit first so that the Universe can show up in full support of your intention.

How does noncommittal instability show up in other areas of life? Let's say you want to run your own business but you work for someone else so you're doing both. If you want real success to show up in your side hustle, at some point you are going to have to quit your day job and leap into the unknown. As long as you show the Universe that you are unwilling to commit to your business by keeping your stable job, the competing frequencies will keep you having to work both.

Both professionally and personally I have seen many people who want nothing more than to work solely on their business idea but they waver, their desire for stability competing with their professional aspirations to build something new. They can't rationalize leaving a secure position for risk and the unknown— so they stay dreaming indefinitely. For me, SMUDGED only became *real* when I left my stable day job. It was scary AF but it was the best decision I ever made. I finally committed fully, despite my (very rational) fears, and it worked out, even better than I thought it might.

Commitment is equal to your actions speaking louder than your words on an energetic level. The Universe doesn't understand your fear, your rationale, or anything else. It only understands your vibe. So get clear. Commit. That's how the good stuff starts to percolate. You can always change paths at a later time.

Belief or hope in possibility can be tricky for the super rational. It is also necessary to reap the benefits of the rituals presented in this book. But you don't have to believe one hundred percent in anything—*nada*. If you choose to shut the door on possibility, then all that is left is impossibility. You just have to leave a door open. Embrace the trifecta—intention, commitment, and belief—and you will be astonished by the beauty and possibility that surrounds you.

Recognize whose lands these are on which we stand.
Ask the deer, turtle, and the crane.
Make sure the spirits of these lands are respected and
treated with goodwill.
The land is a being who remembers everything.
      —Joy Harjo, "Conflict Resolution for Holy Beings"

Before we go further, a note on appropriation and ancestry. Appropriation is understandably a sensitive issue, and a topic I feel everyone would benefit from researching and attempting to understand with an open heart, open ears, and lots of empathy. In short, some folks who work with medicinal plants, many of whom I respect very much, are wary of growing interest in indigenous traditions and rituals from other cultures. Their caution is not uncalled for. In one example of good intentions run amok, wild White Sage has been overharvested for commercial gain by people who have overlooked ethics, culture, and ecological awareness of this sacred planet.

So who am I to be sharing healing plants from various parts of the world? I am an Iranian woman, born in America. I have resided in both countries and have both cultures coursing through my veins. I feel I am just as Iranian as I am American and vice versa, yet I have never been fully embraced by either culture. Growing up, I didn't quite belong anywhere. I was unpopular in elementary school, and by middle school I was being bullied, made fun of, and excluded. Whenever I visit Iran as an adult, I am made aware of how American I am—and again I am reminded that I don't belong. I don't say this for your sympathy, but to emphasize that our roots are both personal and nuanced. Every human you meet has their own complicated story.

You can find Persian people of all faiths—Jewish, Christian, Baha'i—but many of us are practicing, or nonpracticing, Muslims. However, our original religion, that of the Persian Empire before the Arab invasion and Islamization of Iran in the year 641, was Zoroastrianism—a religion based on purity of elemental forces, ritual, and the nature of duality, not unlike Paganism. The Zoroastrian house of worship is a Fire temple. Fire represents excelsior and Universal wisdom, and therefore can never be polluted. It's a symbol of transformation and truth. The central ethics of Zoroastrianism are "good words, good thoughts, and good deeds" and purification is emphasized in Zoroastrian rituals, none of which are performed without the presence of sacred fire. This is the ancestry I connect to most. These are the principles I live by because they feel authentic all the way into my bones.

They are also closely related to the path of modern-day shamanism practiced by my teachers Lena and José Stevens, founders of The Power Path. Everything I've learned about the healing powers of medicinal plants like Tobacco, White Sage, and Palo

Santo, I was taught by these two powerful shamans. For the past twenty-five years, they have aimed to reintroduce shamanic, nature-based wisdom into people's lives.

After one intense ceremony with José and Lena, we had a beautiful conversation about cultural appropriation. My biggest takeaway was that these sacred plants are medicine necessary for the healing of all of humanity; that these practices should be treated with reverence *and* shared, and those are not mutually exclusive. The ancient practices I've learned from Lena and José, so similar to my indigenous religion, have changed my life. They have given me strength and the power to find peace of heart and peace of mind amid chaos. They have given me the stability and freedom to be my most authentic self. Most important, they have connected me to the indigenous peoples of many parts of the world through shared ritual and intention. It is with the humblest reverence that I am here to share the knowledge I have received from my Maman, from my ancestors, and from my teachers, with you.

OPENING SACRED SPACE

Different cultures and traditions open sacred space in different ways, whether that's using angels and allies that are particular to them, or the four directions. Many call in our ancestors. If there is a section of this book that you decide to personalize, let it be this one. The point is to be fully present. It is a space to put aside the human details of life—our to-do lists, our schedules, and whatever else is on our minds. It is a figurative space where we prepare to meet the Divine or Universal wisdom. Within this space, we are able to show up in a more authentic way. And as sacred space is opened, it always needs to be closed through gratitude and acknowledgment of the allies that showed up in support of your intention there.

Again, figure out what feels best for you. Here is what that looks like for me: I always begin by sitting down, closing my eyes, and placing one hand on my heart and one hand on my belly. I take three slow and deep breaths.

I speak my intention aloud or write it down and note *May this ritual be for my best and my highest good.*

I activate the Merkaba Field of Protection (see page 124) around my space, saying aloud that only allies of pure light are welcome. I communicate with Maman and ask for her assistance in opening sacred space and calling forth the angels, allies, and elements that are most supportive of my intention.

I acknowledge and thank Maman, Pachamama, and the other allies I will be working with, like the plants and the element of Fire or Water. Each ritual can change depending on the energies that are present. I light some kind of sacred smoke depending on what ritual I am about to practice, and then begin.

After, I close the sacred space by bowing in reverence,

giving thanks to all of the allies, ancestors, and cultures that contributed.

SPIRITUAL TOOLBOX
AND SETTING UP YOUR ALTAR

I want to reiterate that you don't need much to start working with sacred smoke—matches or a lighter and dried herbs or flowers. You probably already have it all in your kitchen pantry. If a ritual calls for one herb but you feel called to use another, then by all means, do. Making the practice personal and authentic to you is to incorporate your own nuances. Using what you have in your own garden or a neighbor's (with permission, of course) is always preferable to buying something. As I mentioned above, I don't suggest plucking White Sage from the wild because it's being overharvested. (We procure ours from an organic and sustainable White Sage farm in California.) Source local whenever you can. You can almost always find an herb or plant nearby with the properties you need.

Here is a list of all the things I utilize from my proverbial spiritual toolbox, but they're nice-to-haves, not required.

* An altar
* A copper sieve for burning loose herbs over the stove (copper magnifies magic)

* A copper ritual bowl
* Sand to line the bowl
* Dried herbs and flowers for sacred smoke
* Prayer or *mala* beads (in Farsi they are called *tasbee*)
* A physical object depicting any goddesses, gods, angels, or allies you are working with
* Bells and a rattle
* A relic connecting you to your ancestors
* Photos
* Charcoal
* Chime candles in various colors
* Candle-carving tools
* Candleholder and hurricane glass
* Essential and magical oils
* Paper and multicolor pens or markers
* A journal for note-taking
* SMUDGED Cleanse+Protect spray
* Flower essences
* Stone People (aka crystals)—do your best to source them from ethical sellers
* Affirmations
* Tarot cards
* Matches or a lighter

HOW TO SET UP AN ALTAR

First things first, this is not a religious setup. Or rather, while it *can* be, if that is your objective, an altar by definition is not religious. Its purpose is to help you focus on one singular intention. It's a place of devotion. It can be a small table or shelf, a windowsill, or a corner of your room—any place you can create a little space for yourself that can be easily tended to and will be undisturbed by others.

My altar at my parents' home in Los Angeles is my bedside table. As I write this, it holds a white marble statue of Lakshmi Ma, fresh orange marigolds, a few crystals, a rattle, an affirmation, my *tasbee*, and a small brass Ganesha. My altar at my home in Miami is much larger and it takes up an entire corner of an extra room. It's a major part of my living space, but that's not always possible, and not necessary. I've had altars on bookshelves and windowsills. A corner will do.

There aren't any rules when creating an altar—it's just a place that should have meaning for you. It's a space to focus on your true heart's desires. It's a place for introspection and connecting with your higher self. It's a space for transformation, clarity, and magic.

BEST PRACTICES

* Keep your altar free from dust.
* Freshen it up weekly.
* Give it your attention every day by meditating there, praying, or lighting a candle.
* Everything on your altar needs to have a purpose. Make it feel intentional, containing physical representations of what you're inviting into your life and your magical support system. It's a place to create your life like a blank canvas. An abundance altar might include the following:

  * Moolah—bills or shiny coins
  * Anything yellow—like fresh sunflowers
  * Abundance affirmations
  * A physical representation of Lakshmi Ma

* Likewise, for a love altar, try:

  * Dry, organic pink rosebuds
  * Love oil for candle anointing—I use Pratima
  * A red or pink carved candle calling in love
  * Rose quartz crystal
  * Photos or a small vision board of couples whose relationships inspire you
  * Healing, love affirmations

I hope this gets the inspiration flowing to create an altar if you don't already have one. You will quickly find that it is a powerful tool for alchemy.

SAFETY FIRST

With this book, I invite you to live a more ritualistic, nature-based existence, and I encourage you to get curious about sacred smoke, allowing the practices to bring you peace of mind and peace of heart as they have for me and my clients.

When you start bringing herbs and flowers and their essences into your life, do so with caution and reverence. Do research on the plant allies you feel drawn to, taking into consideration not just their healing properties, but also any contraindications and side effects. I love Lavender so much that I want to move to the South of France to live among the purple fields. If I'm ever feeling anxious, I squeeze the *coeur de lavande* that I keep on my altar. With a whiff of the calming scent, my stress melts away. But I can suddenly become sensitive to Lavender, too. I handle it often—it's in many of our products—and usually have zero or minimal reaction, but on occasion I start sneezing and break out in hives. Once, I felt compelled to handle some dried Lavender in a restaurant bathroom and broke out into hives so bad we had to leave the restaurant. My date tried to take me to urgent care. Herbs are powerful!

As you explore and experiment with plant allies, your research should supplement your intuition. Talk to the plants and the flowers. Develop a psychic rapport with them; eventually they start talking back. In the same way I hope you don't blindly adhere to a doctor's advice, be mindful when taking recommendations from an herbalist, a healer, a salesperson—and me, too. We human beings are imperfect by nature, and something that works great for one person may be damaging to another. Take special care when foraging, as look-alikes to common, useful herbs can be harmful. Others are fine for human use but can be toxic for animals.

Once you get comfortable with the plants, herbs, and flowers, you'll learn which ones are calling to you. Louise, the illustrator of this book, grows her own herbs for sacred smoke. When she goes back home to England, she picks Sage, Lavender, and Rose from her family's garden and wraps them with string from her grandmother's sewing kit. She brings these bundles back to Los Angeles and uses them in her practices.

Be like Lou Lou. Grow your own plant allies as much as you can. This way you know what's what and can avoid pesticides. Before picking, I always ask herbs and flowers if it's okay to take them. I do this with shells at the beach and rocks I find while hiking in foreign lands. I always ask permission from nature. I suggest you do too. Your senses will begin to heighten and you will know when the land, or the plant, does not want to share its medicine with you. This is a great way to align your-self with nature.

One more thing before we begin: open the windows! I can't say this enough—you must open lots of windows or have a fierce ventilation system. Not only can smoke from herbs activate allergic reactions and trigger asthma and other respiratory issues, negative energy needs a place to go. If there isn't proper ventilation, it's like sweeping the dirt on the floor from one area to another and never using a dust pan to actually remove it from your space. You'd be shocked as to how many people I have some version of this conversation with:

CLIENT: Is it normal to feel super dizzy after saging your home? Because I've been feeling sick all day.

ME: No, it's not. Can you elaborate? Walk me through what you did.

CLIENT: Sure, I did exactly what you said. I opened sacred space. I invited in my angels and allies and I even called in the four directions. I lit your beautiful wand and walked around my entire home from room to room making sure every corner and closet was exposed to the smoke.

ME: Did you open any windows?

Silence.

CLIENT: Ummm. Was I supposed to? I thought it would be better if the smoke really seeped in.

I also have to give a brief warning about the transformative element of Fire. You have undoubtedly seen the devastation caused by wildfires in California, Australia, and the Amazon in recent years. Never leave burning incense, sacred smoke bundles, herbs or flowers, charcoal, candles, or fires unattended. Never burn anything around flammable substances. The intention behind burning herbs is to release their fragrances and powerful energies. The purpose is not to fill your space, or your lungs, with smoke. A little goes a long way, so burning excessive amounts of any plant ally might lead to respiratory distress and lung issues overall—not to mention that it's wasteful. If your eyes are burning or you are suppressing the urge to cough, you've gone too far. You're either utilizing herbs and flowers that don't agree with you or you're making much too much smoke. Immediately put out whatever you are working with in a fireproof container, make sure the windows are open, leave the room, and put a barrier between yourself and the smoke (like closing the door) until it has completely cleared. Immediately discontinue use and see your doctor if any irritation develops.

Be considerate if you share your space with others. These practices are meant to invite good energy into your life and into your space. If your rituals are triggering another's allergies, or if you live with someone who feels repelled by a specific scent, please show consideration for them. Don't burn smoke around infants, pregnant people, and those whose respiratory functions are limited—like people with asthma, emphysema, allergies, etc.

On that note: Pregnancy can be a contraindication. If you've never worked with sacred smoke before, this is not a time in your life to begin. Herbs can cause miscarriage in women whose bodies are not familiar with their use. If you become pregnant, consider modifying, moderating, or stopping your sacred smoke rituals. Avoid inhaling smoke directly or avoid it entirely. If you are having trouble getting pregnant, consider everything in your environment, even your sacred smoke practices.

The information in this book is offered as just that, information. I can't assume responsibility for the way in which any individual responds to smoke from any herbs or in reaction to any of the rituals herein. I do not claim to be a healer or a physician, so the intelligence contained in this book is not a substitute for medical advice, diagnosis, or treatment. If you choose to burn herbs, always employ your common sense, use in moderation, and don't give your power away to anyone, ever—you know what's best for you.

RITUALS

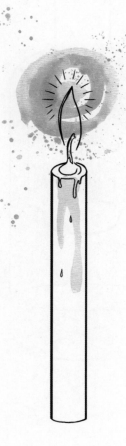

CHAPTER 5

RITUALS FOR SUPPORT

The rituals in this chapter are for when we are in an energy-poor state, which is not a bad thing. It is not uncommon for a person to go through all three energetic states—energy poor, energy neutral, and energy rich—in the same day. This is the business of being human.

When we are in an energy-poor state, we need support because life feels painful and difficult. When we are operating at an energy-poor level, things are challenging and unstable. We're talking breakups, grief, collapse, and stress, so these rituals are for situations when you are in survival mode—to change that frequency, get unstuck, deal with difficult relationships, set boundaries, heal your womb, and more.

The most important thing to remember when you are in this state is that it is temporary, as are all three states. Try to relinquish the need to avoid this state or become too attached to another, because that can cause resistance. Surrender and acceptance of being in an energy-poor state is the quickest way through. We can be sitting in an airplane surrounded by clouds and thunder, amid scary turbulence, but blue skies are just a few feet above. The storm is transient; the beautiful clear blue sky is what's real and ever present.

These rituals will also bring your antenna in alignment with the energy-neutral state, which we'll discuss in chapter six.

GETTING UNSTUCK

If you're feeling stuck in any area of life, call in your allies for the support you need. They're just waiting for you to ask. Lord Ganesha is one of my favorite allies, and I'd recommend you get to know him as well. Ganesha is a Hindu deity who looks like a man with the head of an elephant, with the gentle, humbling, majestic power of that animal. His particular traits and attributes vary depending on which tradition you research, but most agree that he removes obstacles and assigns order to various spiritual powers and abilities. As I've mentioned, I keep a small brass Ganesha statue on my altar. I take him with me every time I travel and I use his mantra daily, humming it beneath my breath when I'm sitting in traffic or standing in line, whenever I'm feeling bored or restless, and always when I walk my pup, Palo.

According to Thomas Ashley-Farrand, author of *Healing Mantras*, Lord Ganesha helps "resolve internal conflicts that you may be projecting onto external situations." He "produces order in the outer world" and brings clarity to our inner world. "The tangible results of this mantra are a sudden, magical disappearance of obstacles," and using it in conjunction with smoke cleansing exponentially increases its power. The results my clients and I have experienced when connecting to Ganesha are astonishing. Give his mantra a try.

Mantra: Om Gum Ganapatayei Namaha (*om gum guh-nuh-puh-tuh-yei na-ma-ha*). The general meaning of this mantra is *Salutations to the Remover of Obstacles.*

* *Om* is the sound of the Universe, used as a greeting.
* *Gum* represents the energy of Lord Ganesha, his *seed syllable* or *bija mantra* (this sound carries his essence).
* *Ganapatayei,* another name for Lord Ganesha. (The literal translation is *spouse of power* because *gana* means *power* in Sanskrit, and *pathi* means *spouse.*)
* *Namaha* means *I offer,* used in mantras as an offering to a higher power.

GRATITUDE

To be in integrity and maintain alignment with your spiritual practices—which also enhances the effectiveness of the rituals—it's always a good idea to give thanks for your materials and pay homage to the cultures whose teachings you are connecting to. So, give thanks to the Hindu religion and any plant allies you wish to use with this mantra.

DEALING WITH DIFFICULT PEOPLE

In 2016, I was hired as Marianne Williamson's head of operations, a challenging and transformational role. After my time with Marianne, I left New York City, where I had lived for almost a decade, and relocated to Florida, where I would later launch SMUDGED.

Starting a company is not easy by any means, and there were people I encountered along the way who presented obstacles big and small. But rather than wishing them harm or hoping they'd leave me alone, I did the very opposite. It's Marianne who taught me this highly effective strategy, from *A Course In Miracles*. She says, "The most powerful way to nullify any negative energy between you and another person is to pray for their happiness. The alchemy is miraculous."*

By praying for someone's health and happiness, you completely transform the relationship. By the end of the ritual, the strife between the two of you will have disappeared or a shift in perception will mean that you are no longer bothered. For optimal results, I recommend practicing this ritual for thirty-three days. The number 33 is a master number in numerology and can lift the self and others into enlightenment.

---

* Marianne Williamson, @marwilliamson, Twitter, September 23, 2018, 4:48 a.m., https://twitter.com/marwilliamson/status/1043829542845132808?lang=en.

WHAT YOU'LL NEED

* A physical representation of the person you are having difficulty with, like a photo or a physical object that reminds you of the person
* Sacred smoke (suggestion: Rose)
* A prayer wishing them well. Below is a sample prayer that you can customize to fit your needs.

Dear Universe,

Please show _____ a clear path to walk today, one that serves their best and their highest good. Send all the angels and allies they need to help them walk this path with grace, ease, and flow. May they feel blessed today. May their heart and their mind be filled with peace. May they feel safe and loved.

Amen. Aho. And so it is!

GRATITUDE

Before beginning this practice, give thanks to Helen Schucman, the original author of *A Course In Miracles*, the plant medicine of Rose, the element of Fire, and, if you wish, to Marianne Williamson for inspiring this ritual.

PERFORM THE RITUAL

1. Sit at your altar with the person's physical representation visible.
2. Ground yourself into Pachamama (page 46) and connect to the Sun.
3. Open sacred space (page 69).
4. Connect to the physical representation of the person. If it's a photo, look at it for several minutes, allowing the image to come alive in your mind's eye. If it's an object, hold it in your hands, bringing it close to your heart. Open up your imagination, using your five senses.
5. Say your prayer aloud, even if it doesn't feel authentic at first—this will change with time.

6. Bring to mind one thing you can find to be grateful for with regard to that person, even if it's something from the past, or a lesson you learned. (If you truly can't think of anything, make any statement of gratitude aloud.)
7. Burn the Rose, allowing the smoke to rise.
8. Close sacred space (page 70).
9. Repeat for thirty-three days consecutively.

In both my clients and myself, I've noticed the crux of personal insecurities are often rooted in societal and familial patterning. And unfortunately, the well-meaning people closest to us, whether that's family, childhood friends, or teachers, can wreak the most havoc on our sense of self.

The Persian culture, my heritage, carries beauty and ancient wisdom, but our community can also be rather dogmatic. School and grades are of the utmost importance. There is a rigorous standard of success coupled with pressure to excel at everything. Not going to college is not really an option, and pretty much everyone has an advanced degree, or three. Iranians tend to be doctors, lawyers, pharmacists, and engineers, and at the top of their field. An emphasis on education and excellence can be a wonderful container of support, but if your personality doesn't fit the mold, it can also feel like a lot of pressure and judgment to fit in. And, of course, different heritages and cultures have their own sets of societal rules that are the lens through which an individual's life and worth are measured.

This can lead to insecurities. For a long time, many of my childhood friends and my closest family members consistently shared with me all of the ways in which I was living my life incorrectly, their concerns that my choices would lead to disaster, that my failure to conform to a linear path was indicative

of imminent failure. The amount of unsolicited advice I've received about everything from my love life to my career path is simultaneously shocking and laughable. A consistent theme well into adulthood was that my very essence made many of the people closest to me uncomfortable. Not surprisingly, that fed the illusion I'd created reactively that something was wrong with me. Perhaps this experience resonates with you too.

I am a Leo, loyal to a fault, but a few years ago I decided to cut the fat. I stopped communicating with the people whose presence in my life created a feeling of lack within me. The question I posed to myself was the following: *Do I feel like something is wrong with me after spending time with this person?*

Sadly, I had to let go of a lot of people. Many didn't understand my desire for space. I was judged harshly—called selfish, weird, and worse. It was disorienting and isolating but also a necessary part of the metamorphosis that transpired. After I started SMUDGED, the fog of insecurities and self-sabotage began to lift. I've come to realize that I'm actually a pretty amazing human being. You are too. Every single one of us is enough, exactly as we are.

Which leads me to our next ritual, The Icebox—a last resort that's ideal for when you feel hopelessly drained by someone else's presence. Or when you have drawn clear boundaries that are being repeatedly ignored. Essentially, relationships involving toxic patterns. You will figuratively be *icing* another's negativity out of your space.

I want to be clear. If you do this ritual and you have any kind of malicious intent toward the individual you're naming, that negativity is going to come back to you with a vengeance. My suggestion is to do some journaling and soul-searching first to make sure that your only intention is to protect yourself, and that you are not in judgment of the person involved, regardless of what has transpired between you both. This ritual needs to be done from a place of love and compassion to prevent any negative implications. In fact, more often than not, just the *cord-cutting* portion is sufficient. I suggest starting there and performing the rest only if necessary.

Your intention should *never* be to harm another. Manipulating someone's free will is dark and not in alignment with being a lightworker. If you need a visual depicting this ritual, imagine you are a home and you're building a fence around your property line, keeping it safe and protected.

WHAT YOU'LL NEED

* About a cup of water
* A sandwich-sized Ziploc bag
* A small piece of paper
* A pen or marker
* A clear intention
* A freezer
* Sacred smoke (suggestion: Wild Rue)
* Optional: a few flowers

PERFORM THE RITUAL

1. Sit at your altar.
2. Ground yourself into Pachamama (page 46) and connect to the Sun.
3. Open sacred space (page 69).
4. Write the person's name on the piece of paper, first and last, and their Sun sign if you know it.

5. Hold their name in your hand and send them thoughts of love, compassion, and understanding. Forgive them regardless of fault. The forgiveness is for your peace of mind, not to let them off the hook or pretend it didn't happen.

6. Burn a bit of sacred smoke and imagine cutting any energetic cords connecting you to this person. If it feels good, ask Archangel Michael to help or imagine his bright sword cutting the cords.

7. Put the piece of paper in your Ziploc bag. I always add some fresh flowers for sweetness and to invite light and compassion in.

8. Say your intention aloud. Make sure it's positive. Sample intentions:

   * My intention in doing this ritual is to bring myself peace and protection.
   * My intention is to protect my space.

9. Then pour water into the bag until the piece of paper with the name is submerged.

10. Let the air out, making the bag as small as possible, and seal it. I do my best to make sure their name is straight and hasn't accidentally been creased.

11. Fold the bag around the name and place it in the back of your freezer. Leave it there—without going back to check it or mess with it in any way. Just wish the person well, send them light every time they cross your mind, and

forget about it. (A couple of years from now you will be cleaning out your freezer and happen upon the bag and be surprised at how such strife resolved itself.)

12. Wash your hands and burn more sacred smoke. Say something to the effect of:

> Dear Spirit of Wild Rue (for example),
>
> Thank you so much for your beautiful cleansing energy. Please let any lingering negativity between _____ and myself dissolve. Please cleanse and protect my space and bring me into alignment with my best and my highest good. Amen. Aho. And so it is!

13. Wish the same for the person you are having difficulty with. Then wash your hands and you're done.
14. Close sacred space (see page 70).

> ## GRATITUDE
>
> Don't forget to give thanks to the herbs, flowers, the element of Water, and any other plants or allies you've used.

RITUAL FOR DEEP REST

Rest is the most underrated form of self-care. So much so that in this age of constant go-go-go, getting adequate rest can be considered radical. I am good with my ritualistic commitments but I almost never get enough sleep, which over time is hard on the body. Not sleeping enough can lead to:

* Memory issues
* Lack of concentration and inability to focus
* Moodiness
* Being accident prone
* Weakened immunity
* Increased risk of heart disease and diabetes
* High blood pressure
* Low sex drive
* Fluctuations in weight, increased BMI
* Poor balance

I had an epigenetics interpretation of my DNA done by a wellness coach and my biggest takeaway was about my sleeping habits. Epigenetics is a study of how your unique DNA patterns interact with your environment, like diet and exercise habits, stress level—and sleep. My epigenetics coach Lindsey told me I need eight and a half hours of sleep a night to function optimally.

I laughed out loud because if left to my own devices I'm the type
of beast who maxes out at *maybe* six hours.

But I knew that not resting sufficiently is a form of self-
sabotage and neglect so I decided to try giving my body the
sleep it needed for a month as an experiment. For thirty-three
days I went to bed no later than ten p.m. each night and woke
up at six-thirty a.m., no snoozing allowed. My life changed

considerably for the better. I was more productive, less stressed, and more joyful overall. I didn't experience my normal day-to-day mood swings and I barely noticed when my period arrived that month. It also helped me get more out of my morning routine. I felt so much more connected to my practices, not at all like I was just checking things off a to-do list. I was able to sit in meditation longer, with less fidgeting.

I use a parasympathetic breathing technique to soothe my nervous system right before bed. The autonomic nervous system—divided into sympathetic and parasympathetic—is the branch of the nervous system that carries out the vital functions of our major organs without conscious control, like circulation, lungs, heart, and glands.

The sympathetic nervous system helps our bodies gear up for physical exertion by increasing heart rate, blood pressure, sweat, and pupil dilation, while the parasympathetic nervous system slows everything down in preparation for digestion and rest. Both systems react unconsciously to physical activities like exercising, sleeping, or eating, or mental stimuli like stress or meditation. Breath also stimulates the nervous system. By altering the ratio of our inhalations to exhalations, we can adjust sympathetic or parasympathetic activity in each breath cycle. Specifically, exhaling for longer than you inhale facilitates deeper relaxation because it extends the period of parasympathetic activity with every breath. It takes attention away from the sympathetic system, which stimulates the body, and focuses on the parasympathetic nervous system, which promotes relaxation.

During my thirty-three-day, eight-and-a-half-hour sleep experiment, just before bed I would light some Palo Santo because the scent calms me, and with this holy smoke wafting around me I would begin this breathing technique. All you have to do is allow your exhalations to be twice as long as your inhalations. Start with two counts in, four counts out. The following night try three counts in, six counts out, until you find the rhythm that works best for you.

After a few rounds I would put the Palo Santo out and get into bed, continuing this breathing technique until I floated off to sleep. On the nights that you employ this ritual, you will sleep restfully and wake up feeling refreshed.

GRATITUDE

Remember to give thanks to your lungs for allowing you to employ this breathing technique. In fact, take a few moments to do a quick body scan and feel gratitude for your whole being, especially for all the cells and organs that work 24/7 to keep you healthy without any conscious effort. Also, always give thanks to any herbs you burn for sacred smoke.

WHEN YOU NEED A DO-OVER

Of all the words of mice and men, the saddest are, "It might have been."

—Kurt Vonnegut, *Cat's Cradle*

In Albert Einstein's general theory of relativity, the flow of time is regarded as malleable and conditional. Many spiritual teachings share the sentiment that time is an illusion, merely a construct of *this* three-dimensional earthly plane. It seems real to us because we live in and through time. But its nature is illusory. That's why sometimes an hour feels really long and other times a whole day goes by in a flash. With this perspective, we can influence time to transform our lives for the better. One way is by choosing to revise past decisions and actions to alleviate remorse.

Regret is a useless emotion—one that keeps us tethered to the past. In fact, it's a waste of energy that borders on delusion. Every choice we made was the right choice, and the only choice, whether or not it led to our desired outcome. Our nuanced history, wounds, intelligence, conditioning, and many other factors led us down a certain path and the decision we made was the best we could do at the time. It can seem like there was another path we could have taken, but that false belief is the root of a tremendous amount of suffering.

While I genuinely feel like there are no wrong choices, I'm also imperfect and human, so on occasion, there are life happenings that don't sit right in my skin. You know those moments where you disconnect from yourself for a split second and end up doing or saying something that causes damage and alters the course of your life? Ugh, just writing that creates knots in my stomach—it's been a while but I know the feeling well.

Well, since time is a construct, this ritual carries the power to go back and energetically change and neutralize any negativity and regret. You can go back to a specific decision or action or conversation—and choose differently. Whenever I've practiced this exercise, the knots in my belly unfurl, and peace of heart and mind wash over me.

For the ritual, it's best to focus on one moment in time and fully release it before revisiting another incident, on another day. Begin with any bigger situations you might be harboring from the past and then move to smaller ones. Pick up your journal and consider the following prompts, writing a short paragraph for each.

* What are some regrets living in your mind that you'd like to release?
* How often do you contemplate these regrets?
* What would you do differently if you could go back in time?
* How would your life look different if you had a redo?
* Which has the biggest charge? Start with that one, let's go.

WHAT YOU'LL NEED

* A memory you are ready to do over
* A quiet place

* A clear intention of why you want the do-over and how exactly you would choose differently
* A glass of water
* Sacred smoke (suggestion: Thyme)

PERFORM THE RITUAL

1. Sit at your altar.
2. Open sacred space (page 69).
3. Take a few rounds of deep belly breaths until you feel settled in your space.
4. Invoke your intention aloud, or quietly to yourself.
5. Bring the memory to mind with as much detail as possible—going back to that specific moment in time.
6. Envision yourself making a different choice. Saying the different thing. Or just walking away. Visualize it, and choose differently. What would you say, do, not do? How would you handle yourself with grace? And then just do it—in your mind's eye. Neutralize the situation with the simplest, cleanest possible reality.
7. Burn your sacred smoke, allowing the smoke to rise around yourself—remembering the illusive nature of time and reminding yourself that this exercise isn't just figurative.
8. Sit for a few moments in silent meditation.
9. Drink your glass of water.

10. Close sacred space (page 70).

11. Repeat as needed (but no more than once a day to avoid overwhelm).

Most days, I do an abbreviated version of this ritual before I go to bed because the results never cease to amaze me. It completely transforms the dense energy of resentment and the past going awry. I scan my day for little regrets. Any moments I wish I had behaved more mindfully. Did you make any decisions you wish you could take back? Any words you wish you hadn't said? Do you need a *redo*? Anything, at all, you wish you had handled differently? When you practice this daily, it becomes about little things, and the process takes under ten minutes. Repeating this exercise daily is not only spiritual maintenance but it keeps me more mindful in general. Over time I have experienced many fewer moments I feel the need to redo.

GRATITUDE

Remember to give thanks to the element of Fire and the herbs you have burned. Also send Namaste energy to the person or people who were mentioned in your ritual.

WOMB HEALING

Losing a baby is a heart-wrenching reality many of us have experienced. The specifics of the loss are not as important as the fact that it transpired, and this ritual is appropriate for anyone who has suffered the loss of a child—especially those whose babies were born sleeping, and women who have miscarried or terminated their pregnancies. The first part of the ceremony is appropriate for partners as well. This practice is a process of acknowledging and honoring your child's existence, thereby integrating their soul into your life. It will serve as a passageway to true acceptance and healing.

Life happens. Being human is not easy or fair. When it comes to pregnancy, we are sometimes faced with choices we might not feel prepared to make, while other times the decisions are made for us and we have no say. It can feel easier to shut off and move on—or maybe the sorrow or the grief or the guilt permeates our core. No matter how strong our nature, a person who has experienced the loss of a child needs healing and support, which the first part of this ritual will facilitate.

The second part is about connecting to and cleansing our feminine essence and is appropriate for the person whose body carried the fetus.

In some cultures, it is said that the womb is our second heart center, which resonates with me. We are connected to our ancestors in more ways than we are cognizant of. Just consider the fact that you were in your grandmother's womb as a teeny follicle when your own mother was growing as an embryo. So we hold the collective joys and pains of our lineage through our maternal line. All of the women in our family, in both this life and in past ones, are interwoven. When we heal ourselves, we simultaneously heal our ancestors. A pattern is released.

Many women don't connect with our anatomy in a way that supports the release of energies that no longer serve us. Our uterine energy is the source of our power but it usually goes unnoticed—unless we are experiencing our menstrual cycle, and

then our attention focuses more on complaint or nuisance than reverence.

For this exercise, I will refer to the female reproductive organs—including our uterus, fallopian tubes, vagina, accessory glands, and external genital organs—as the *sacred bowl*. This physical and energetic space rests at the root of your body, the sacred space in which you experience physical and energetic merging and exchange with a lover. This practice will help clear out any grief, trauma, and blockages so you can reclaim residency there, connecting you to and igniting your feminine power.

Our sacred bowl is viscerally receptive. When you receive a lover, it is a physical, emotional, and energetic exchange. Some of us are skilled at shutting off our emotions as a defense mechanism, so the experience might seem different, but most of us are aware that receiving someone into your body is much more than a physical act—it's a state of vulnerability.

This same idea applies to a life growing within your uterus. No matter how brief the pregnancy, or the stage of development, or how long ago it was, being pregnant changes the very nature of our being. While there are countless reasons why you may not have been completely in residence with your sacred bowl to begin with—upbringing, trauma, violation, shame, or a simple lack of awareness—a failed pregnancy can exacerbate this separation. This ritual will bring attention and nourishment to this critical place of beauty and power in our bodies and heal all that needs it.

This is a heavy topic, and possibly a triggering one for you. Do the work anyway—the deeper the wound, the more profound the healing. Connecting with your uterine energy is an essential part of accessing the divine feminine and the energetic state of reception. If for whatever reason you don't have a uterus or other feminine reproductive organs, focusing on the region will have the same effect, as the energy still exists.

WHAT YOU'LL NEED

FOR PART 1

* White taper or chime candle
* Carving tool for the candle; a safety (or bobby) pin will suffice
* Paper and pen
* Recommended: An altar with a glass hurricane candleholder in the center surrounded by fresh flowers and a photo or ultrasound of your child (if you have one and only if it feels good to see it, not if it generates angst)

FOR PART 2

* A quiet space to lie down
* Moonstone crystal is ideal but not necessary
* About fifteen minutes of uninterrupted time

* Sacred smoke (suggestion: Angelica and Rose)
* A full glass of water
* Recommended: The most powerful time of the month to perform this ritual is on consecutive days from the New Moon until the Full Moon, but any day or length of time you make space to connect to your sacred bowl is perfect.

PERFORM THE RITUAL, PART 1

1. Sit at your altar.
2. Open sacred space (page 69), calling in your female ancestry. Include language that invites in light entities only; for example: *Female ancestors of one hundred percent light, from my maternal line, hear me now. If you wish to come forth in support of this ritual, I invite you in.*
3. Place your hand on your womb area and connect to your lost baby. If your partner is present, ask them to sit behind you and place their hands over yours. I am not going to include specific instructions on how to connect to your child because it will be different for everyone. Just know that a clear intention, spoken aloud or in your heart, is enough. You can't do this wrong, so trust innate wisdom. You will undoubtedly feel the connection when it's been made.
4. Spend a few minutes at least, and as much time as you'd like, feeling the emotions that come forth. Try to stay out of

judgment and your rational mind as much as possible to facilitate catharsis. If you are doing this with a partner, it would be best to hold space for, but not physically or verbally comfort, each other at this point in the ritual. This may feel counterintuitive because we are societally programmed to hug someone, pat them on the back, say it's okay, or interrupt in some way when emotions begin flowing forth. While there is no ill intention, it disrupts and sometimes blocks the emotions that are coming up for release. It may be uncomfortable, but try to wait to offer physical and verbal comfort until after the ritual is complete.

5. When you feel complete, pick up the candle and carve your baby's name into the wax. If you didn't name the baby, do so now. If you don't feel called to name the baby, that's okay, too, you can simply write *baby girl, baby boy,* or *baby.* Carve anything else you feel called to and place your candle upright in the hurricane.

6. Take your paper and pen and write a letter to your baby, or anything else you are called to write. If you are doing this with a partner, it would be best for each of you to write your own letters. Write from your heart without editing or rereading, like a stream of consciousness. The only important thing to do in the letter is to acknowledge the life that was once inside you. That is the true purpose of this ritual—acknowledgment.

7. When you are done, fold the letter(s) and place them under the hurricane—making sure the candleholder is flat and secure so there is no fire hazard. If your letters are so thick that it makes the base unstable, place them anywhere on the altar, or skip the fold.

8. Light your candle in acknowledgment of this life.

9. Sit for a few moments staring at the flame in silent meditation.

10. Close sacred space (page 70).

11. For forty days leave the remnants of the candle and refresh the altar with fresh flowers or herbs from your garden. On the fortieth day, release the letter into nature with devotion—don't hold on to it. You can burn it and spread the ashes in a place that brings you joy and comfort, or bury the pages, including any bits of the candle left over from the ritual. Consider planting a tree sapling in that spot as well.

PERFORM THE RITUAL, PART 2

1. Lie down in a comfortable position.

2. Place your moonstone over your womb.

3. Place your left hand over your heart and your right over the moonstone on top of your womb area.

4. Breathe deeply and slowly for eleven rounds, activating the parasympathetic breathing exercise (page 100) and releasing

everything but the present moment—your to-do list, worries, thoughts—calling home all the parts of yourself that might be with others, back to your heart. Gather all of you, even the bits that are connected to those you love—your pets, children, and/or partner—so that you're whole and completely present.

5. Bring your attention to your sacred bowl. Can you shrink yourself and imagine being inside your womb area? Make that your intention even if your mind says it's not possible. Just spend some time here, connecting, feeling, being in your sacred bowl.

6. Start walking around. Explore. Notice the texture, the temperature, variances . . . Are there areas with cobwebs? Where is there light? Where is there collapse? Imagine clearing or sweeping and tidying up, maybe bringing in flowers or burning sacred smoke. How about lighting a candle? Try different things. The point is to simply connect and take up residence in your own feminine sacred space.*

---

* If you've never done an exercise like this before, it sounds *super weird*, and the first few times you might feel numb, or like you're unable to access your sacred bowl. That's perfectly normal—most of us don't even have full control of our pinky toe. Keep at it, because the experience will shift dramatically with a bit of patience. The aim is to feel like you're coming home to a sacred space. It usually takes a couple of weeks to really access this part of yourself, maybe longer if you have experienced intense trauma. No matter what, I promise that you will benefit greatly from repetition of this practice.

7. When you have explored a bit, sit for a few moments in silent meditation.

8. When you feel complete, sit up and drink your glass of water.

9. You might want to journal about anything that came up for you.

10. Cleanse your moonstone with sacred smoke as soon as possible. This will facilitate release of any trauma and blockages transferred to the crystal.

11. Close sacred space (page 70).

GRATITUDE

There are so many things you can feel gratitude for in closing this ritual. Please give thanks to the things that feel authentic to you. Here are some ideas: the crystals and any tools you used during the ritual, your body (especially your sacred bowl), any allies and ancestors that came forward in support, the element of Fire, any sacred smoke you used . . .

NEW YEAR RELEASE

An ideal time to do this ritual is on the last Full Moon before the end of the year, but any Full Moon will do. For us to move forward both in our personal lives and to create societal transformation, we cannot be stuck in lower vibrational frequencies. As I've mentioned before, it's not that change cannot happen when in a lower energetic state, it's just that it's a lot harder and there is a lot more effort involved—like doing jumping jacks with boots on, in the mud. This practice will release any negativity that you might be feeling from the holidays and from the past year.

WHAT YOU'LL NEED

* Paper
* Pen
* Copper sieve
* Metal tongs
* Fire
* Sacred smoke (suggestion: Mistletoe, White Sage, and Holly)
* Pomegranate seeds (optional)

PERFORM THE RITUAL

1. Sit at your altar.
2. Ground yourself into Pachamama (page 46) and connect to the Sun.
3. Open sacred space (page 69).
4. Call into mind any gunk you're feeling, whether it's issues you're having with other people, or anxiety over finances, or feelings of lack or fear. Let go of feelings like impatience, procrastination, depression, anything that's pulling you down. Give yourself three to five minutes to write down everything that is troubling you. Let it flow; don't edit or reread or check spelling or grammar. Let go of perfection and trust that this will work and that what needs to change, will.

5. Without reading back over the list, close your eyes and connect to the lower vibrational energies that you want to release. Dig deep. The aim is real tears—no pressure if that doesn't happen, I just want you to open up to and allow your feelings to flow.

6. Call in your allies and angels in assistance to release that which no longer serves.

7. Rip the paper into smaller shreds that will be easy to burn.

8. Take the copper sieve and shreds of paper into the kitchen, making sure you have windows open (proper ventilation, always!). Burn the pieces of paper in your sieve right over your stove. Use tongs if it's too hot. The element of Fire is transformative, able to transmute negative energies to neutral ones. Burn it all until it's ash. If a tiny piece doesn't burn, it's not a big deal, as our aim is never perfection.

9. Discard the ashes by releasing them into the ocean or toilet, or by spreading them in your garden.

10. Now that you've released this negative energy, make a promise to yourself that you will not engage in low vibrational actions like complaining, gossiping, or rumination. When you start going in that direction *stop* and quickly shift your focus—turn up some music, call a friend, or move your body. You want to let the transmutation settle in rather than connect again to the memories you have set in motion to release.

11. You've created a neutral space. A blank slate. Say aloud your intentions for calling in things like health, happiness, love, joy. Burn a pinch each of the White Sage, Mistletoe, and Holly to facilitate.

    In Persian (and Greek) mythology, pomegranates symbolize fertility, beauty, and eternal life. Since they are ripe in the winter, I enjoy pomegranate seeds after doing this ritual and especially on New Year's Day to connect with the energy of the fruit. If you feel called, I invite you to do the same.

12. Close sacred space (see page 70).

GRATITUDE

Remember to give thanks to the element of Fire, the herbs you have burned, the pomegranate seeds, and any other elements and allies who showed up.

CHAPTER 6

RITUALS FOR COMFORT

The following rituals are for when we are energy neutral. When a person is in this state they are in alignment with the status quo. It's nice to *not* be in a state of fight or flight, but I've got to be real: your comfort zone is where dreams die. These practices are for when you are ready to get a bit uncomfy, because to be uncomfortable is to grow into a more energy-rich state. They include protecting your space, everyday cleansing, blessing the new, calling home the lost, rituals for abundance, self-love, and more.

SACRED GEOMETRY FOR PROTECTION

Mathematics is the alphabet with which God has written the Universe.

—Galileo Galilei

I always did pretty well in school, but math was never my strong suit. The only class I ever had to repeat was geometry (my left-brained parents were mortified). But if someone had explained to me the sacred nature of mathematics, and geometry in particular, I would have paid better attention in class. Maybe.

What is sacred geometry? In her book by the same title, Miranda Lundy says, "Sacred geometry charts the unfolding of number in space. It differs from mundane geometry purely in the sense that the moves and concepts involved are regarded as having symbolic value, and thus, like good music, facilitate the evolution of the soul."

In simpler terms, sacred geometry describes geometrical laws that are responsible for creating everything in existence—it is the underlying order of the Universe. Sacred geometry represents the unification of science and spirituality. It's my happy place.

Everything in nature—including the human body, segments of a flower, even a beehive—is made up of geometric patterns. Each of these patterns carries a unique energetic vibration, which creates a frequency. The same mathematical ratios that

are found in cosmology are also found in music, light, architecture, and art. It's a unifying structure that connects every facet of the Universe. It's the fabric of *everything*.

Meet your new bodyguard—the Merkaba. Use it for daily protection of all kinds. Pair it with an ethically sourced black tourmaline crystal and you will be untouchable—truly shielded. This sacred geometric character is made up of two tetrahedrons—three-dimensional triangles. It's a symbol of balance and stability because each side lies flat no matter how you turn it. The tetrahedron also represents the element of Fire, which adds to its powers of purification, and it links the spiritual and physical worlds. The Egyptian pyramids are one example of a tetrahedron, and many crystals, like agate, citrine, and hematite, too. It is depicted in Islam as the Seal of Solomon, and in Christianity as the Holy Trinity; it is also central to Judaism, as the Star of David; and some see it in Leonardo da Vinci's *Vitruvian Man*. This symbol also has sacred significance in Hinduism, Buddhism, Jainism, the Church of Jesus Christ of Latter-day Saints (or Mormonism), the Rastafarian movement, and Paganism too. Don't be surprised if you start seeing the shape everywhere now.

Back to the Merkaba. You can see that the tetrahedrons are pointed in opposing directions—one toward the sky, channeling energy from the heavens, and the other toward the Earth, drawing up the grounding nature of Pachamama. This starlike shape brings together divergent energies—masculine and feminine, Earth and cosmos, light and dark—integrating them into balance. It is a physical representation of our personal power when we are similarly in alignment.

How can we use this symbol in our daily lives? The answer lies in the root meaning of the word. In Egyptian, the word *merkaba* translates to *light, spirit, body,* and in Hebrew it means *chariot.* The combination of the two depicts its unique structure as a vehicle, or symbol, of protection. So how do we activate this vehicle of protection and how can it help us in our daily lives?

I call upon the Merkaba daily. I imagine drawing it, usually in an electric blue light, around myself, Palo Santo (the doggy, not the wood), my loved ones, my company's logo, this book, the Uber I'm about to step into, my luggage before checking it, packages before they are sent out, my laptop, my phone, my home, my plants, stray dogs and other random animals (in real life and on the Internet), on airplanes before I take off, and definitely before I get into the ocean because I'm irrationally afraid of sharks. You name it, I've used it. In fact, I activate it so often sometimes I force myself to take a break because I don't want to become superstitious about it, or anything. (Superstition is a fallacy, and connecting to it dilutes the energy of whatever ritual you are doing. It's the wrong vibe altogether.)

WHAT YOU'LL NEED

* Your imagination
* The Merkaba
* Sacred smoke (suggestion: Frankincense and Myrrh)

PERFORM THE RITUAL

I usually do this in the morning as part of my daily practice, and sometimes throughout the day as well. You don't need to go through every step below, and you don't even need the sacred smoke—you can activate the Merkaba at any time, no tools necessary. The steps will just lend structure to your first time activating the symbol and in case it feels good to have a ritual supporting its use. I know plenty of people who have benefited from this practice.

1. Sit at your altar.
2. Ground yourself into Pachamama (page 46) and connect to the Sun.
3. Open sacred space (page 69). Call in any of your allies.
4. Visualize yourself in your mind's eye.
5. Draw the symbol around your space (or whatever/whomever you are wanting to protect) in electric blue light.

6. I use my hand, or fingers, to draw two opposing triangles in the air because that helps me visualize it. You don't need to use anything if you don't need it. Don't forget it's a three-dimensional shape.

7. Repeat as necessary.

8. When you feel complete, close sacred space (page 70). Thank your allies and get on with your day.

9. Repeat as needed.

GRATITUDE

This practice is so ancient that I'm unsure of a specific culture or person to thank for inspiring it. How about thanking yourself for showing up, for committing to raising your frequency, and for showering yourself with some much-needed love and attention? Don't forget to thank the elements and allies who showed up as well.

EVERYDAY CLEANSING

After a good night's rest, our minds are like fresh sponges ready to absorb information. The things we introduce into our consciousness first thing in the morning direct our attention and path for the day, so being particularly mindful in the mornings is essential for how your day, and therefore your life, will unfold. For this reason, I recommend that before you go to sleep, you put your phone on airplane mode and don't take it off until you finish your morning rituals.

In the same way the strongest trees have the deepest roots, grounding allows us to root ourselves into Pachamama so that we are protected energetically. Grounding in the mornings and also connecting to the Sun anchors our energy to something positive and supportive to set the tone for the day ahead (page 46). From an evolutionary standpoint, our bodies are designed to wake up with the Sun and our brains have specific receptors that respond to sunlight, letting us know it's time to get going. So wake with the Sun as often as you can. This entire exercise should ideally happen before even looking at your phone or any artificial light. Go outside and connect to the energy of natural light. If it's freezing cold outside, you can just open all of the curtains and fill your home with sunshine.

Next, burn some sacred smoke or spray a cleansing room spray and bless your space. I suggest you choose one herb, flower,

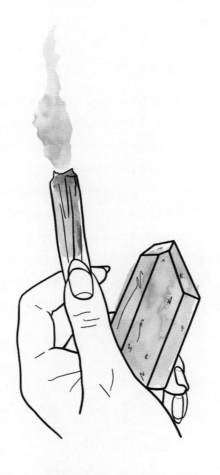

or spray to work with for at least two weeks to familiarize yourself with its energy and how it can cleanse and protect you. Ask to be guided by connecting to your higher self. Take a few minutes to journal for any clarity you might need. As always, remember to feel grateful for the allies and elements who support you in your everyday cleansing.

BLESSING THE NEW

I cleanse and protect the inanimate objects I bring into my life. I bless everything from clothes and electronics to journals and skin care products. Just think about how much energy is lingering on the shoes you picked up at the mall, for example.

Blessing the new can be as simple as taking a few breaths and grounding yourself into Pachamama, connecting to the Sun, and then opening sacred space. Once you've done that, burn any sacred herb you feel called to, letting the smoke waft around your new purchase. Open your heart to feeling grateful for the item and to all of the people, and plants and animals who contributed

to creating whatever it is that is now in your possession. The ritual below can be used for anything—if you just bought a car, there's a more specific ritual for that as well.

WHAT YOU'LL NEED

* Sacred smoke (suggestion: Calendula)

PERFORM THE RITUAL

1. Ground yourself into Pachamama and connect to the Sun (page 46).
2. Open sacred space (page 69).
3. Set a clear intention to cleanse and protect your item.
4. Burn your sacred smoke.
5. Close sacred space (page 70).

GRATITUDE

Give thanks to the medicinal plants and herbs you used, and to the spirit of Fire, as well as to all who helped create your new belonging.

BLESSING A NEW VEHICLE

Persians have a lot of little traditions I grew up with and love. I learned a version of the following ritual the first time my parents bought a brand-new car when I was in middle school. A few months later, my mom was driving the car when it hydroplaned on Topanga Canyon, a narrow, winding, two-lane road, during a terrible storm. Her two back tires were teetering off the edge of a cliff. She had to be rescued, but she (and the car) were just fine.

Ever since, each time I've gotten a new car, or for that matter anyone I've known has, I've performed this ritual. The car doesn't have to be brand-new—just new to you. It's always kept the drivers and passengers of the car safe, even in serious accidents and perilous situations. Over the years, I've altered it slightly to add more protection and magic.

The left side of the body is the receiving side, so we place an egg under the left side of the vehicle, allowing the blessings, support, and protection to link to the receptive state. The shell of an egg is hard and protective. It shields a developing life from the dangers of the outside world, and its magical use similarly shields people, animals, and objects against the dangers of the outside world. The materials we use carry their own energy so it's important to make sure no animals are being harmed by your ritual. When procuring an egg, I urge you to find a local, non-commercial farm and do your research. Harming other

living creatures, in any way, will affect the integrity and the efficacy of your ritual and intention.

The Zohar is a book of Kabbalistic teachings and a tool for protection from illness and danger. The pocket-sized version mentioned here is a one-volume edition containing the section that deals with healing, with an introduction in English, Spanish, French, Chinese, Japanese, Farsi, and Russian. I have one in my car, my purse, and all of my luggage.

WHAT YOU'LL NEED

- ✳ One egg
- ✳ Sacred smoke (suggestion: Wild Rue)
- ✳ A pocket-sized Zohar

PERFORM THE RITUAL

1. Ground into Pachamama and connect to the Sun (page 46).
2. Open sacred space (page 69).
3. Set a clear intention to protect your vehicle and all the beings that might use it and cross its path.
4. Burn Wild Rue, allowing the smoke to cleanse both the egg and the Zohar.

5. Burn more Wild Rue outside, allowing the smoke to cleanse the inside and outside of your vehicle.

6. Place the egg behind the back left tire, and drive over the egg in reverse.

7. Place the Zohar in the glove compartment.

8. Close sacred space (page 70).

GRATITUDE

As I've mentioned before, it's important to give thanks while performing any ritual—in this case, to the Persian culture, Kabbalistic teachings, the spirit of Wild Rue, and the element of Fire. Also, give thanks to the chicken whose egg you've utilized. Honoring the animal will foster harmony and connection, creating a stronger container of support for your ritual.

CALLING HOME LOST ITEMS

Some things just like to be lost.

—Louise Androlia

I lose things more often than I'd like to admit. Keys in the freezer. Cell phone in the hamper. Palo's leash in a box full of Sage. Laptop in airport security. My sunglasses, even when they are on my face. So when I came across these statistics in a recent

article, they really struck a chord: we misplace up to nine items a day, and spend much of our precious time (up to fifteen minutes a day, or two and a half days a year) searching for random articles we've mindlessly lost track of. It's not just losing your keys when you're rushing out the door for an important meeting, or chasing after the phantom ring of your cell phone (*yes*, you already looked for it in the couch cushions).

It's that these little losses can bring up emotions about the impermanence of, well, everything, and that emotional component seems to cause just as much chaos as the literal misplacement. Even if you later find the item, losing things brings into clear focus the fact that your life isn't as organized as you thought it was, that sometimes you lose control despite your best efforts, and that someday, just like that book you never managed to locate, you're going to be simply a memory, too.

These sentiments bring us to my number one go-to ritual— how to call the lost home. I have a busy personality and a long to-do list, which leads to many not-so-mindful moments. On top of that, my anxious attachment style makes it difficult for me to lose things, so I use this ritual frequently. Lucky for me, it works every time.

My mother taught me this practice when I was a kid. (Clearly my absentmindedness goes way back, although I swear I'm getting better, if only because of my practiced nonjudgmental attitude regarding this aspect of my personality. Remember:

releasing shame and guilt about parts of ourselves we wish were different is absolutely life changing.) When I asked her about the root of this ritual, she shrugged, paused, and then said, "I don't know, it goes back hundreds of years." I added the sacred smoke element as an adult because I have found the transformational element of Fire speeds things along; you may choose to skip that part, though.

I have since found similar rituals in Turkey, Greece, among Iraqi Jews, Cubanos, and of course my witch sisters. I feel such peace when I learn that so many cultures employ similar practices. It's a gentle reminder that we are all more connected and similar than our superficial differences.

WHAT YOU'LL NEED

* Something to tie. A piece of string works fine.
* Sacred smoke (suggestion: Rosemary)

PERFORM THE RITUAL

1. Ground yourself into Pachamama (page 46).
2. Open sacred space (page 69). Call in any allies.
3. Visualize finding your lost object and invite in the sensations you know you'll feel once reunited. Employ your five senses with as much detail as you can muster. Can you feel

the object in your hands? What are you doing with it? What will you be using it for? The more you can connect to the joy, pleasure, and relief of finding it, the faster this spell will work.

4. Focus on your heart space and cultivate as much gratitude as you can muster for your object. Fill your being with appreciation, love, and awe.

5. Tie three knots in your piece of string, making sure you can untie them once you have found what is lost.

6. Place the string somewhere safe. I always leave it on my altar.

7. Finally, burn your Rosemary or other herbs and allow the aroma to boost your mood and jog your memory.

8. When you feel complete, close sacred space (page 70). Thank your allies and just get on with living. Do your very best to completely release the need to find the object. Simply allow the magic to unfold.

9. When your lost item is found, make a commitment to take better care of it and untie your string.

GRATITUDE

Don't forget to give thanks to the element of Fire, Rosemary, any other herbs you've used, the string, and of course your allies. And please send my mama (her name is Sheedeh, which means *bright like the Sun*) a little love too, for sharing this practice with me. Good juju is always welcome, and much appreciated, in our family.

ALIGNING WITH ABUNDANCE

I was initiated into Unitarian Reiki by Chilean reiki master Isabel Vial and her sister Bárbara. This branch of reiki consciously utilizes sound, color, and sacred geometry as a tool for personal and Universal healing. Its purpose is to bring us into alignment with our own inner master, divinity, and wholeness through restoration of patterns of "perfect" physical, mental, emotional, and spiritual health.

There is one Unitarian Reiki symbol that can be shared with everyone, even if you're not initiated into the modality, and that is the Symbol of Abundance. Working with this symbol can affect both our material and spiritual abundance by unlocking latent potential. It assists us in calling forth prosperity into our consciousness and into our lives by activating and expanding the abundance and prosperity already in and around us.

Just looking at the symbol will spark its juju, but it's even more powerful to draw it in your mind's eye. I envision it over my computer when I'm writing, and I imagine it over my company's logo, and whenever I'm about to walk into a business meeting or taking a work-related call. There are a myriad of ways to use this symbol, and it's also the perfect companion to working with another ally, Lakshmi Ma.

Lakshmi Ma is the Hindu goddess of prosperity in both the physical and spiritual realms. She is pure magic. To invite

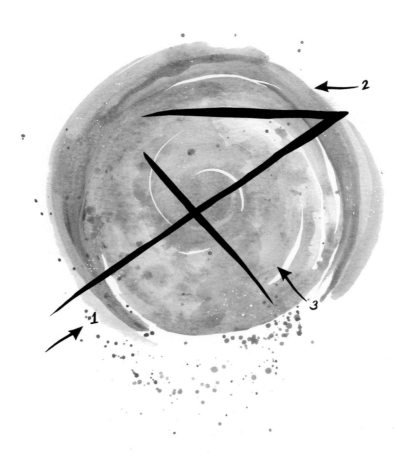

Lakshmi into your heart is to welcome in love, beauty, and riches. It is said that when you chant the Lakshmi mantra 108 times a day for forty-four days, abundance will be yours.*

I adore Lakshmi Ma and I offer up prayers to her daily. She has brought so many blessings into my life (and those of my clients as well)—including the very book you're holding. In late January 2020, I decided to push myself and finish the book proposal for *The Art of Sacred Smoke*. I'd been sitting on it for a while and my agent was patiently waiting for me to finish.

I started a forty-four-day practice with the intention of procuring a competitive book deal with a major publishing house. I asked Lakshmi Ma to make the process quick and uncomplicated. This is no easy feat, especially for a first-time author. I didn't even mention it to anyone out of fear of being laughed at. I worked night and day on the proposal and a couple of weeks later, I had a decent draft submitted to my agent, who helped finalize it and sent it to a mix of publishers. I received positive responses in less than twenty-four hours and soon after had calls set up with about a dozen publishers. Then, with what felt like lightning speed, my publisher made me an offer I could not turn down.

---

* Why forty-four days? There are many ways to do this ritual and forty-four resonates most with me because of its numerical significance. Angel Number 44 is a magnification of the number 4, which brings mind, body, and soul together with the physical reality of structure and organization. It's a number of support and stability that invokes a grounded nature in things. In this case, it takes the ethereal nature of the Lakshmi mantra and grounds her abundance into your physical reality.

In just five weeks, I went from not even having a finished book proposal to signing the exact deal I'd asked the Universe for. This is the magic of Lakshmi Ma. And that's just one example. I have many.

I'm sure you're ready to try this out for yourself but there's more to aligning with abundance. The most important thing is tuning in to the state of reception. Receptivity is a state of mind. It is the opposite of doing and forcing and pushing. It is a space of possibility, of openness and surrender. Usually when my clients are stuck in lack, when they are feeling hopeless, anxious, or overwhelmed about finances, they are also disconnected from the receiving state.

In fact, I cringe a little when I hear people saying things like *no days off, rise and grind,* and *success is born of struggle.* It is true that you won't likely amass abundance without work and determination—Lakshmi especially is said not to favor the lazy—but adopting a struggle mentality in which you believe your willingness to sacrifice or suffer is in direct correlation to your success is programming that will keep you stuck in lack.

Basically, don't expect to sleep in and watch TV all day, every day, then chant the Lakshmi mantra and rake in a million dollars. At the same time, be cognizant of your programming and mentality. If you believe rich people are cunning, or that you must suffer to find abundance, or if you were taught that money is the root of all evil, it would behoove you to release those core beliefs. It doesn't need to be a huge undertaking or take a long time to transform those patterns, and recognition is the first step. Consider hiring a coach, therapist, or teacher who can guide you—but first release any blockages with regard to wealth.

Next, you want to connect to the state of receptivity, which is the exact opposite of making an effort—it's a space of flow. There is little or no manipulation, ego, or force behind your desires and actions here. One thing that helped me tremendously is this prayer by Tosha Silver:

Divine Beloved, Allow me to give
with complete ease and abundance,
knowing You are the unlimited Source of All.
Let me be an easy, open conduit for
Your prosperity.
Let me trust that all of my own needs are
always met in amazing ways
and it's safe to give freely as my heart guides.
And equally, please let me feel
wildly open to receiving.
May I know my own value, beauty and
worthiness without question.
Let me allow others the supreme pleasure
of giving to me.

May I feel worthy to receive in every
possible way.
Change me into One who can fully love, forgive,
and accept myself . . . so I may carry your Light
without restriction.
Let everything that needs to go, go.
Let everything that needs to come, come.
I am utterly Your own.
You are Me.
I am You.
We are One.
All is Well.

I say this prayer every single morning because it brings me peace, and I use it in conjunction with the Unitarian Reiki Symbol of Abundance. Tosha's words remind me of my innate power and help me step into a state of reception, so the actions I take each day are more aligned with my best and my highest good. This prayer helps me stay out of ego and fear with regard to business and it serves as a gentle reminder that I am wholly supported by the Universe—I just have to be willing to step out of my own way. The greatest changes in my life have arisen from this state of vulnerability and openness.

This abundance trifecta—the Unitarian Reiki Symbol of Abundance, Tosha's prayer, and the forty-four-day Lakshmi ritual—will create a supportive foundation for your efforts with wealth and abundance. I'm so freaking excited for you to start! Are you ready to try it out for yourself?

WHAT YOU'LL NEED

* 108-bead *mala*
* A quiet place
* A clear intention of what you want to draw into your life
* Mantra: Om Shreem Maha Lakshmi Ya Swaha (*om shreem ma-ha lak-shmi yah swa-ha*)
* Sacred smoke (suggestion: Cinnamon, Jasmine, and Saffron):*
* Optional: An altar with a physical representation of Lakshmi Ma and fresh flowers for her. I leave her marigolds because of their gold color and because I've been told that in India, the flower symbolizes auspiciousness and is offered as a symbol of surrender and trust in the Divine.

PERFORM THE RITUAL

1. Sit at your altar.

---

* I prefer Cinnamon with a sprinkle of Jasmine and Saffron. Cinnamon raises your consciousness to the frequency of abundance. Jasmine calls forth a natural force of attraction. And each Saffron thread must be handpicked from the flower so it's the most expensive spice on the market. I use just a bit to bring a sense of opulence to the ritual. As always, you are welcome to improvise and use whatever herbs and flowers you feel drawn to.

2. Open sacred space (page 69) and greet Lakshmi Ma, inviting her into your heart.

3. Invoke your intention aloud, or quietly to yourself.

4. Burn your sacred smoke, allowing it to rise around you and your depiction of Lakshmi if you have one.

5. Repeat the mantra 108 times, keeping count on the *mala* beads.

6. Sit for a few moments in silent meditation.

7. Close sacred space (page 70).

8. Repeat for forty-four consecutive days.

GRATITUDE

Remember to give thanks to the Hindu religion, Lakshmi Ma, the element of Fire, your *mala* and any other allies who supported you in this process. Thank the sacred herbs, flowers, and anything else you feel called to thank. If you are working with the Symbol of Abundance or Tosha's prayer, give thanks to those teachers as well.

SELF-LOVE MIRROR EXERCISE

Unconditional love is a natural craving of all human beings. Many of us readily show love and appreciation for others—our children, spouses, significant others, friends—while perhaps not experiencing this type of love in return (except from our pets). Even our self-talk can be abusive. Since we can't control how others love us, or other people's behavior in general, learning to truly love yourself is essential to mental and emotional well-being.

Mirror work is transformative. It can also feel weird and uncomfortable at first. Doing it anyway, despite the discomfort, will allow you to begin shifting the relationship you have with yourself. In time, you will begin viewing yourself through the lens of unconditional love.

Next time you pass a mirror and make eye contact with yourself, try asking, *What's up, gorgeous?* It will probably make you smile or even laugh—bringing out a little happiness and joy from the inside. And when you're ready to deepen your practice, try the following ritual:

WHAT YOU'LL NEED

* A full-length mirror
* Sacred smoke (suggestion: Chamomile)

* Privacy
* Optional: music

PERFORM THE RITUAL

1. Open sacred space (page 69).
2. Stand or sit in front of your mirror, preferably naked. If the thought of being naked in front of your mirror terrifies you, start in a bikini.
3. Look into your own eyes, for at least a minute—literally just gaze into your eyes.
4. Say out loud, *I see you. You're beautiful. I love you.*
5. Burn a bit of sacred smoke and watch as the smoke wafts over your skin, blessing you, showering you with love from head to toe.

After a few days of doing this, when you begin feeling comfortable with the routine, move on to showering yourself with more affection and appreciation. Some ideas:

* Talk to yourself about how proud you are of a certain accomplishment or how you handled a situation that week.
* Start looking at the different parts of your face and body, cultivating appreciation for every single inch of you.
* Practice self-love during your skin care routine by mas-

saging your face and including *afformations** like "Why is my skin glowing?" or "Why am I so radiant and beautiful?"

Mirror exercise allows us to embrace our own essence and true nature. It's a way of getting completely comfortable in your own skin. With repetition, you will see your relationship with yourself and your self-perception shift completely. When practicing, stick to whatever gets you connected to the reality of *you*—a pure, graceful, courageous being.

If you're feeling like you need an extra boost of energy, dance in front of the mirror completely naked. Put on a song or a mantra that makes you feel alive and beautiful. Make eye contact with yourself and *feel* your soul. Sing. Dance. Howl. And shake it out.

GRATITUDE

Remember to give thanks to the element of Fire, the sacred herbs you've burned, and of course yourself.

---

* An *afformation* is an affirmation posed as a question. I learned about them from a man called Noah St. John when I felt affirmations weren't working for me no matter how much I tried. The concept is a subtle but powerful twist—by turning positive statements into *why* questions, the subconscious mind doesn't have a chance to block the thought and instead it looks for answers. It circumvents that bitchy back talk you might experience when using affirmations.

CHARSHANBEH SOORI—SPRING EQUINOX FIRE-JUMPING RITUAL

I love the spring and I think I've made my affinity for Fire clear by now. In the Iranian tradition, on the eve of the last Tuesday before the spring equinox, which is also the Persian New Year, we gather to jump over fire as a ritual of release and transformation. All you need is the element of Fire. If you live in an area with a lot of Iroonis like Los Angeles, you can do an Internet search for beach bonfires on that day and just show up. My people are very welcoming and someone will show you what to do! If you don't live around a lot of Iroonis, make a bonfire in your backyard in a fireproof firepit, or even use a candle, which is what I did for the years I lived in New York City. I would put a candle on the floor (securely—please don't burn your apartment down) and jump over it. While jumping over a big bonfire with lots of other people carries a stronger charge, doing *something* is so much better than doing nothing and this is one of the simplest rituals you can do to heal and transform.

First, I recommend a thorough spring cleaning. Before this eve, go through all of your drawers and closets and give your home a Marie Kondo–level refresh. Keep only that which sparks joy, and as you go, repeat this mantra: *I am cleaning out the closet of my mind*. The clarity that comes from this simple act alone mystifies me every year.

After the cleaning, before the jumping, journal with these prompts. Dig *deep*. The more you are willing to delve into your psyche, the greater the changes for the positive.

* What fears are blocking you from going all the way in your life?
* Identify where you are thinking small or in a limited way.
* Where are you afraid to face pain?
* In what ways is pain controlling you?
* Identify your ego of jealousy or competitiveness.
* What is your area of laziness?
* Where are you holding on to resentments?

These are not easy questions. Good for you for answering. You can bring your answers to the bonfire if you'd like to burn them. It's up to you—keep what you need, discard the rest.

Now, the ritual. Find your communal bonfire or create one legally and safely. When you are ready to jump, first say the following:

Sorkhi-e toh az man
Zardi-e man as toh

What you are saying is *Give me your beautiful radiant glow and take from me my sickly pallor.* This is an ask from the Fire.

Jump twice, once each way, and say this as you jump. Give everything that no longer serves you to the Fire and take in the blessings.

I hope you have a beautiful Charshanbeh Soori. Enjoy.

GRATITUDE

Remember to give thanks to the element of Fire, to Persian people in general (and Zoroastrians specifically) for sharing this tradition, and for any sacred smoke you may have used.

Allow the fires of transformation to burn away all that doesn't serve you.

—Heather Ash Amara

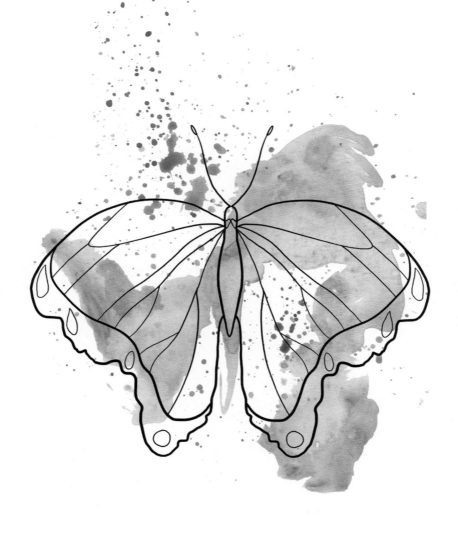

CHAPTER 7

RITUALS FOR PROGRESS

The rituals in this chapter are for when we are experiencing an energy-rich state and are in synergy with that awakened mode. This beautiful, blissful mood is not sustainable long-term, because it's not a grounded state of being, so it's difficult to get things done in an earthly manner. Nevertheless, it feels the best of the three states of being.

When we are energetically rich, we are able to give to others and raise consciousness, affecting change with ease, because we feel good and connected to Universal intelligence. It's a state of benevolence and empathy. The energetically rich state is the opposite of fight-or-flight. We are filled with peace and everything feels like it happens almost magically.

The rituals outlined in this chapter are to support leveling up, both on a personal and spiritual level. They include rituals for chakra balancing and alignment, sending healing and abundant energy, creating Future Imagined Memories, blessing others, understanding the nature of love, and connecting to your higher self. This space is connected to thriving, feeling hopeful, and aligning with the receptive state—overall it's a place of balance. The most important thing to remember when you are in this state is not to get attached because like everything else, it's temporary.

CHAKRA BALANCING AND ALIGNMENT

This ritual will keep your energy and your vibration high, and it will help you remain balanced when performed regularly. If you're unfamiliar with the chakra system, think of chakras as the energy centers of your body, from the base of your spine up to the crown of your head. The seven chakras are interconnected, so when one is experiencing imbalance or blockage, all of them are affected. This energy system is real and can wreak havoc on your mind, body, and spirit when its equilibrium has been compromised. Tuning your chakras is like tuning an instrument or a vehicle. Regular maintenance is required for optimal function and is essential to a life of flow and release from suffering.

The first chakra is called the root chakra or Mūlādhāra and is depicted by the color red, the Earth element, and yoga pose

Virabhadrasana II. All of the rooting exercises in this book begin at this point of the body. The developmental stage attributed to the root chakra is from the womb (pre-birth) to twelve months, and Cedar is its closest plant ally. This chakra is associated with survival, stability, security, and our basic physical and emotional needs. It is the figural foundation of your life force. Imbalance and blockages manifest as anxiety disorders, depression, fear, worry, overthinking, emotional/physical disconnection, rage, nightmares, panic, and instability.

The second chakra is called the sacral chakra or Svadhisthana and is represented by the color orange, the element of Water, and the yoga pose Baddha Konasana. It fuels creativity, and its associated developmental stage is two to three years of age. The plant allies best suited for this chakra's health are Gardenia and Damiana. The sacral chakra is connected to the realm of emotions and is associated with sensuality and sexuality. It is our pleasure center. Imbalance and blockages of this chakra manifest as guilt, addiction, sexual dysfunction, codependency, and relationship issues.

The third chakra is the solar plexus or Maipūra and is associated with the color yellow, the element of Fire, and the yoga pose Dhanurasana. This is your power center. Developmental stage—eighteen months to four years. Plant allies: Saffron, Musk, and Sandalwood. The solar plexus determines your dominant personality. It is the place in the body that controls willpower, self-worth, and authenticity. The third chakra is connected to digestion and your *gut feelings*, and if it's out of whack, it manifests as insecurity, difficulty making decisions, lack of self-control, and misuse of power.

The fourth chakra is called the heart chakra or Anāhata and is connected to the color green, the element of Air, and yoga pose Camatkarasana. Unconditional love is rooted in this chakra. Developmental stage—six to twelve years. Its plant allies are Jasmine, Lavender, and Rose. The heart chakra is connected to love of the self and others. It is the home of compassion, empathy, charity, and the *we* versus *I* mentality. The fourth chakra is responsible for flow and balance in giving and receiving. Imbalance and blockages here manifest as resentments, an inability to let things go, shallow interpersonal connections, lacking empathy, and isolation.

The fifth chakra is the throat chakra or Visuddha and is associated with electric blue, the element of Ether, and the yoga pose Simhasana. The expression of the authentic self begins here. Developmental stage—seven to twelve years. Plant allies: Chamomile and Frankincense. This chakra, which is ruled by the planet Mercury, is all about communication, expression, and manifestation. Issues here take root as social anxiety, dishonesty, fear of expressing oneself, stubbornness, and defensiveness.

The sixth chakra is called the third eye or Ajna, and is connected to shades of deep blue or indigo, the element of Light, and the yoga pose Savasana—the final pose at the end of a yoga class (or sequence) that serves as the integration of the physical and metaphysical planes. This is your house of intuition. Developmental stage—adolescence. Plant ally: Mugwort. The third eye is connected to self-awareness, foresight, clarity, and equanimity. Impediments here manifest as confusion, illusory perception, problems concentrating, and an inability to see the Truth, with a capital T.

The seventh chakra is the crown chakra or Sahasrāra and is connected to the colors violet, pure gold, and iridescent white, and the yoga pose Vrikshasana. It relates to the cosmos or Center Universe. All of the grounding exercises in this book culminate here. Developmental stage— spans throughout every age of life (and it's especially active later in life). Plant ally: Myrrh. The crown chakra is associated with enlightenment, bliss, and Universal oneness. Any imbalance here manifests as close-mindedness, attachment, constant cynicism, and a disconnection from Spirit and/or the physical body.

Now that you know a bit about the chakra system, infuse this knowledge with the following ritual, as you connect to each of the seven and uncover what may be out of alignment or blocked. Once you are cognizant of any negativity or imbalance, you can shift the energy and access the positive attributes of each chakra.

CHAKRA-BALANCING STONES

 Root chakra stones: ruby, red jasper, or garnet—focus on clearing and balancing, not opening

 Sacral chakra stones: carnelian, tangerine quartz, or orange moonstone—focus on clearing, opening, and balancing

 **Solar plexus stones:** yellow jade, citrine, or brucite cluster—focus on clearing, opening, and balancing

 Heart chakra stones: rose quartz, jade, green calcite, or green tourmaline—focus on healing, opening, and balancing (always needs clearing)

 **Throat chakra stones:** kyanite, lapis lazuli, turquoise, or aquamarine—focus on clearing, opening, and balancing

Third eye stones: amethyst, fluorite, or iolite—focus on clearing and opening. When your third eye chakra is too open—and most people will not run into this imbalance—you will be taking in too much information from others (think *cosmic trash can*) and it will not serve you, so keep this in mind if you're highly sensitive.

Crown chakra stones: selenite, clear quartz, or Herkimer diamond—focus on clearing and balancing, not opening

A NOTE ON CLEANSING
AND PROGRAMMING CRYSTALS

Too many of us pick up crystals at the store and use them without cleansing or protecting them properly. This makes me cringe. When you connect to Stone People, they carry the energy of every single person who's used or held them, until they reached you, or were cleansed by someone else.

If you want the crystals you choose to be your allies and in alignment with your energy, you must cleanse and program them. You can do this by using sacred smoke (any of your herbs will do), bathing them in the light of a Full Moon, soaking them in the ocean, or spraying them with a protective spray. Be mindful, as some crystals, like selenite, are water soluble, so no salt water or spray on those, please.

Next, program your crystal, because intention is everything and your ally needs direction to assist you. Take a few moments and contemplate the properties of the stone you have chosen. Consider: What do you need right now? How can this crystal be of service to you? And then with clear intention, program it.

Hold the stone in your left hand, because that is the receiving side of the body. Program your crystal by succinctly and firmly, but with gratitude and reverence, telling it how it will be responsible for helping you. Clearly state the support that you need.

PERFORM THE RITUAL

1. Ground yourself into Pachamama and connect to the Sun (page 46).
2. Open sacred space (page 69).
3. Lie down and place cleansed and programmed crystals on your body in correspondence with the chakras.
4. Close your eyes and focus on your tailbone, placing your hand over your root chakra. Bring your attention there. Are you feeling any fear about survival? Are you experiencing

feelings pertaining to things that might feel specifically dangerous? If your root chakra is vibrating with fear, or a low frequency like despair, this chakra needs to be cleared. Focus on accessing the energy of vitality instead. You can do this through your connection with Pachamama. Put your attention again on your first chakra and feel it as a vibrant disc of red energy. In your mind's eye, see it opening temporarily to eliminate what's no longer needed by your system. Is there anything in there right now that is keeping you in fear or despair? Envision it draining out of your root and into Mother Earth. Ask her to transmute your waste into fuel and love for herself. She will receive the energy you don't need, recycle it, then send it back up your root as health, vitality, and positive energy for you to integrate. Imagine this in your mind's eye. If you have trouble envisioning it, speak it—your intention will suffice. Sound is powerful and facilitates transformation, so make any noises you feel called to.

5. Take a deep breath and relax your torso.

6. Now move your attention up to the second chakra, the sacral chakra, and bring your focus there by placing your hand to your lower belly. This is the home of your sexuality and creativity. It's also the place of destruction, irritability, and rage. While they may seem like competing energies, they are two sides of the same coin. If you are feeling any of the symptoms denoting imbalance, focus

there to transmute the negative energy into creativity. See this chakra as a sphere of bright, fiery orange light between your hip bones. Make any noises you feel called to—sound assists in transmuting anger into creativity.

7. Shift your attention to the solar plexus, just above your belly button, placing your hand over your third chakra. From this place in your body, your overall energy is distributed. It is responsible for how you show up in the world. If you are feeling confused, stuck, or powerless in any way, it needs to be cleared. Picture this area as the Sun, literally. Envision bright yellow blasting through any imbalance or blockage. Make any noises you feel called to, to support elimination of stagnancy in this chakra.

8. Once it feels clear and balanced, take a deep breath and relax your chest.

9. Now, focus on your heart (not your actual heart but the center of your chest), placing your hand over your fourth chakra. Your emotions are not actually held here. This chakra holds the energy and information about experiences we've had that have not yet been cleared from our system. We integrate our life lessons here. Growth happens here. Always cleanse your fourth chakra to assimilate past experiences and be receptive to the new; whatever is coming your way will be blocked if this chakra isn't in optimal condition. Make any noises you feel called to when healing, clearing, and assimilating the

emotions held in this chakra. Tending to your heart chakra daily is an act of self-love and self-care.

10. When the process feels complete, take a deep breath and relax your neck and shoulders.

11. Move your attention to the little soft space at the hollow at the front of your neck. Focus on your fifth chakra to communicate your heartfelt desires and express your unique creativity through your voice. You can speak, sing, tone, or just make sounds. When you do this with intention, the sounds you make will clear and balance your throat chakra and support your thyroid. Don't be shy; make the noises you feel called to. This is how you can learn to speak your truth with compassion.

12. When the chakra feels clear and balanced, take a deep breath and relax your face and jaw. Massage your mandible with your fingers or a *gua sha* stone.

13. Focus on your third eye, which sits in the middle of your head behind the bridge of your nose. Bring your attention inward behind your eyes. From here we can connect to our inner knowing. When I do this, I feel a pulsating sensation. You might see colors, feel tingling, or pressure, and your eyes will most likely flutter. Ask aloud for your allies to help you see that which you cannot see with your physical eyes. This is the place of your intuition, inner knowing, and inspiration. Allow the coolness of the crystal on your forehead

to connect you to your third eye, clearing confusion between the perception of others and your own. Imagine filling your headspace with the color indigo and make any noises you feel called to, in support of release and catharsis.

14. Finally, focus on the crown of your head—your seventh chakra, which represents a small funnel that receives information from all around and can access multiple dimensions. Bring your attention here, to your spiritual portal—your human antenna. The crown chakra will connect you to downloads from your guides and allies that you might otherwise miss. Some people envision this chakra as violet in color; I see it as a pearly, shimmering, iridescent white light—whatever you picture is fine. It's not necessary for this chakra to be open unless you are purposely accessing it in meditation or wanting to communicate with your guides. (If that is the case, then you can open the crown chakra with your intention, as well as toning. Sound in particular facilitates opening and clearing of this chakra.) Be especially cautious about leaving it vulnerable if you are a sensitive person because you will feel overwhelmed and even assaulted by other people's energy, especially if you're in a busy city. Clear your seventh chakra now by toning, and when you feel complete, imagine covering it with a filter—a bubble, pattern, or sacred geometric symbol that will keep out unwanted energy.

15. Take deep breaths and imagine a light source from Center Universe beaming straight through each of your chakras in a straight line, connecting and aligning them—like the way you'd sit up straight to lengthen your spine. Start with your crown chakra, then your third eye, your throat chakra, your heart chakra, solar plexus, sacral chakra, and finally your root chakra.

16. Next, bring in that vital life force from Pachamama through your root chakra and mix the grounding energy of the Earth with the ray of light coming through your chakras from Center Universe. Perfect! You are now supported, aligned, and grounded.

17. Daily repetition is ideal.

GRATITUDE

Remember to give thanks to Pachamama, and to any crystals and sacred smoke you used. Also, to the chakras, colors, elements, and anything else you connected to during this ritual. The more gratitude you cultivate, the more effective your rituals will be. Appreciation is always the magic ingredient.

My friend Kristen Joy, one of the funniest, most beautiful, smartest women I know, and founder of Voluptuous Life, taught a group of us this Eye Shakti ritual at the beginning of the COVID-19 lockdown in March 2020. Many of the teachings come from ancient palm-leaf manuscripts taught to Kristen by her guru in India.

She and I became friends around 2007 when I was training her to take over my role at a hedge fund in New York City. (What very different lives we both had!) Even though we've

lived on different coasts the majority of the time we have known each other, we remain close friends, and thirteen years later, she continues to inspire me. The first time Kristen led me through this ritual, it was such a profound experience, I asked her to lead the SMUDGED community through the process as well. She's been gracious enough to let me share *my* version of this teaching with all of you, so send some love her way before you begin. And drink plenty of water afterward. Think lubrication— water not only makes shift happen, but it also helps your body release any energy that comes up for release.

The Eye Shakti means *eye power*. So, this ritual is a simple and effective practice of sending healing and abundant energy to others using the eyes, and the second part diffuses any negative or lower frequencies you may be carrying. The transformative nature of this practice seems to build over time. It only takes about ten minutes so this ritual can easily be incorporated into your routine.

WHAT YOU'LL NEED

* A photograph of whomever you'd like to work with, whether that's a person, pet, ascended master, angel, or deity. Whether the soul is still in their body or has passed on doesn't matter. It can even be yourself. You must be able to clearly see their eyes in the photo.

* A physical representation of the element you feel called to work with. A houseplant might represent Earth; a lit candle, Fire; a bowl of rosewater, Water; and your breath, Air.

PERFORM THE RITUAL

1. Sit at your altar with your photograph clearly visible.
2. Open sacred space (see page 69) and make sure your electronics are turned off.
3. Connect to your heart chakra—what is your intention for this practice? Make it clear and concise without attaching to a particular outcome. Boundaries are essential when connecting to the space of another without their express permission. While many of us think we might know what's best for someone else, are convinced that we see their flaws and methods of self-sabotage with perfect clarity, we are in fact clueless. I doubt we are generally clear on what's best for our own soul, much less that of another.

Here are examples of high-vibration intentions for this practice:

* *I'm sending you love, light, and protection for your best and highest good.*

* *In alignment with your best and your highest good, may the challenges you're facing resolve with grace, ease, and flow.*
* *May your heart and your mind be filled with peace, may you feel safe, blessed, and loved.*

4. Employ Kristen's Box Breathing meditation and imagine forming a cube of safety around yourself. In your mind's eye, draw the lines of a box while you:

   * Breathe in for four seconds through the nose (side one).
   * Suspend the breath for four seconds (side two).
   * Exhale from your mouth for four seconds (side three).
   * And finally, hold your breath again for four seconds (side four).
   * Repeat for several rounds.

5. Begin the Eye Shakti ritual by looking at the photograph and gazing into your subject's eyes.
6. Chant Om Nama Shivaya (*om nah-ma shee-vah-ya*) as you send *maitri* from your heart to theirs.

* *Om* is the sound of the Universe—it is used as a greeting.
* *Nama Shivaya* together calls forth Lord Shiva—a representation of the Universal oneness of the five elements.
* *Maitri* is also known as *metta*. It is a feeling of loving-kindness, of benevolent affection toward another. While the practice of *metta* is an essential part of Buddhism, it is open to use by people of all faiths (and no faith) because it is a tool to elevate our collective consciousness.

7. Continue chanting at an interval that feels right to you for a minimum of three minutes and a maximum of eleven minutes.

8. Close the practice by bringing your hands to touch at your heart center and then chanting Om Shanti Shanti Shanti (*om shan-ti shan-ti shan-ti*), which is an invocation of peace. We repeat *Shanti* three times to depict peace within the mind, in speech, and of body.

   For the second part of the process, state your intention. Examples of some high-vibe intentions for this discharge are:

* *I connect to the element of Fire to transmute any negativity in my space or being into positivity and light.*

I call forth the element of Air to transform any negativity stored in my being into positivity.

9. Finally, neutralize any charge brought on as a result of performing the Eye Shakti ritual.

10. Connect to the element you've chosen and its physical representation:

    * Touch the dirt of your houseplant representing Earth.
    * Watch the flame of your candle dance to connect with Fire.
    * Dip your fingers in your bowl of rosewater to connect with the element of Water.
    * Close your eyes and feel the inhalation and exhalation of your breath upon its entry and exit to connect to Air.

11. Once again, chant Om Nama Shivaya (*om nah-ma shee-vah-ya*) as you send yourself thoughts of peace and love.

12. Continue chanting this mantra at an interval that feels right to you for a minimum of three minutes and a maximum of eleven minutes.

13. Close the practice by bringing your hands to touch at your heart center and then chanting Om Shanti Shanti Shanti (*om shan-ti shan-ti shan-ti*)

14. Release the charge from the element you utilized by first expressing your gratitude and then supporting each elemental representation in the following ways:

* Houseplants can transmute negative energy the same way Pachamama does. So take a moment to ask the dirt to transform any negative charge in your space into fuel and love for the plant.
* Allow the candle to burn out in a fireproof container.
* Pour the rosewater back into the Earth or down the drain.
* Feel gratitude and focus on your breath as the element of Air is sufficient for the process of discharge.

GRATITUDE

Please give thanks to my friend Kristen Joy for sharing this process. Consciously feel gratitude for the being you worked with, any elements you used, allies, ancestors, and angels that came forth in support of this ritual, and the Indian culture for passing down this sacred practice and for the powerful mantras recited.

FUTURE IMAGINED MEMORY (FIM)

This ritual is all about manifestation—a word I used to abhor because of its frequent overuse, abuse, and incorrect usage. But manifestation is something we do all the time, albeit unconsciously, so it's time to reclaim the word and give it a deserving ritual to boot.

One of the most transformative things you can ever begin doing is to delve into your imagination regularly and start *thinking in pictures*—of what you love, of what you want, and who you dream of becoming. It's less about the specific image you conjure up and more about getting lost in the feeling of living the life of your dreams. Connecting to the energy of joy, happiness, excitement, and peace will call forth those things when you align with their frequency. Recent scientific research has concluded that our brains are unable to differentiate between an actual memory and something that we have imagined lucidly with all of our five senses. And since our future is largely dependent on past

experience and the notion that our thoughts become things, imagining a particular moment in the future of our choosing sounds like a great practice. Right? So let me introduce you to the concept of a Future Imagined Memory (or FIM).

I was introduced to this technique over a decade ago by my South African fairy godmother, Donna McCallum. A FIM is like a story we tell ourselves in the present tense about the outcome of a specific desire or goal. It's a make-believe tale about the future, a time when your dreams have become a reality. Donna suggests writing your FIM out clearly, describing the experience in as much detail as possible, utilizing hearing, taste, touch, smell, and sight. Getting detailed about the five senses is the secret sauce to help elicit the emotion necessary for this exercise to be successful. I like to record myself so I can listen to the story daily. It helps me envision the whole thing unfolding, like watching a film.

I've done this practice many times and its track record still shocks me. Is your rational mind reeling right now? I get it. But consider that if in 2019 I had told you that within a year, life as we knew it would completely shut down globally. That we would all have to quarantine and wear gloves and face masks to protect ourselves from the spread of a deadly virus. You'd probably have laughed and judged me silently, or even questioned my sanity. Whatever the reaction, there is *no way* the bizarre reality of the COVID-19 pandemic was a possibility in your consciousness a year before it transpired.

The truth is, we have no idea what is possible in this life a year from now, or even next week. Our limited brains run on an operating system rooted in past experiences and societal programming. But there are infinite possibilities, realities, and paths available at this moment, many of which seem absurd or impossible. If the pandemic taught us anything, it's that *anything* is possible. A Future Imagined Memory can connect you to a possibility beyond your present circumstances; that is its power. So, imagine what good can happen a year from today, or three months from now. Don't just dream big—allow this practice to open you up to dreaming *huge*.

Contemplate a life that holds the same degree of absurdity as an international pandemic, but a positive version. If it's wildly unreasonable, absolutely illogical, and makes you feel like reality is bending, while it simultaneously makes your heart light up and gives you butterflies, it's possible! If it weren't, you wouldn't be able to conjure it up. So, dream it. Then dive in with your five senses and empower yourself to live a little—or a lot—differently.

Get ready to be amazed.

WHAT YOU'LL NEED

* A piece of paper and a pen or pencil
* A recording device—I use my cell phone

✳ Sacred smoke is optional (suggestion: Palo Santo and Angelica for opening and closing sacred space; Wild Rue when burning your FIM)

PERFORM THE RITUAL

These first three steps you will only perform once, when creating your FIM. The rest of the steps will be a daily practice.

1. Write out your FIM, making sure you include descriptive moments that touch upon each of the five senses.
2. Record yourself reading your FIM, leaving pauses for your imagination to flow.
3. Burn the paper with a little sacred smoke if you wish, offering up the ashes back to the Earth.
4. Put your phone on airplane mode.
5. Open sacred space (page 69).
6. State your intention for this FIM, reminding yourself of your dream or goal, aloud or silently in your heart.
7. Play back your FIM, listening carefully and allowing yourself to feel all of the feels.
8. Close sacred space (page 70).
9. Repeat this listening practice consecutively for forty days, no more, no less.

10. When finished, try not to think about your FIM again and have full faith that the Universe will provide exactly what you've asked for—or better.

BEST PRACTICES

* Keep your FIM under ten minutes long so that you don't feel overwhelmed when listening to it daily.
* Keep your story the same—the recording helps with this. Don't add or take away details because that will take away from the daily repetition. Maintaining the same story ingrains it into your memory.
* Ignore the *hows*. Create the story around an outcome and not how you arrived there. For example, if you want to write a book, it's unhelpful to imagine yourself on your computer for the daily grind. Instead, imagine your launch party, being interviewed about the book, or seeing it on the shelf in a bookstore.
* If your FIM isn't as clear as you'd hoped it would be, don't stress. You're not doing it wrong.
* Most of us have one or two senses that outshine our others—you can thank your unique neurolinguistics programming. So, for many people, visualizing a dream in our mind's eye is nearly impossible. The aim is an overall sen-

sory experience. Try not to worry about doing it correctly, what's most important is that you are doing it.

* Distraction is normal. Just as in meditation, our minds can wander or we may become distracted. Gently bring yourself back into the story and continue—and this will probably happen a few times. You're good, so try not to make a big deal out of a little distraction.

* Get comfy. Spend a few minutes in the mornings or evenings jumping into your FIM. Lie down and get comfortable, but stay alert.

* Imagine yourself in the scene, conjuring up excitement.

* The more you enjoy the sensations and positive feelings associated with your Future Imagined Memory, the more effective this ritual will be.

GRATITUDE

Remember to give thanks to Donna McCallum, the element of Fire, and the plant allies you're burning. Give yourself some love for showing up to do this transformational work.

NAMASTE—MAY YOU ALL BE BLESSED TODAY

Namaste *creates vibrations to the one receiving the gesture.*
Namaste creates a loop of bliss to pass positive energy on to
the one receiving the gesture. Heart centers and chakras are
said to connect during the divine saying.

—Isabelle Marsh, MindBodyGreen

Are you familiar with the word *namaste*? It's a respectful greeting
to another, a reverent hello.

Since energy is real, we can bestow namaste to others without being face-to-face. No matter how far the distance, this ritual fosters an openhearted connection with the people who

cross your path, whether it's those you exchange energy with daily or those whom you may not even have noticed. Practicing namaste also enriches those relationships you already nurture. Performing this ritual will create remarkable shifts in your relationships with family, friends, and coworkers, and boost your overall magnetism.

In the morning, as a part of my daily practices, I share namaste energy with everyone I might interact with that day. It is a heart-opening way to start your day, and if you try it you will notice a subtle shift in how you are treated by others. People will begin to receive you differently, as you will be more magnetic, and while they might not understand it with their rational mind, the effects are tangible. It's also fun to sing *Namaste Namaste Namaste. May you all be blessed today.* What started as a song I would sing to my doggie when he'd paw me because he felt ready to go out and I was still doing my morning rituals has turned into a jingle I sing a lot. I can be out and about in the car or on my bike, and whenever I cross paths with someone, in my head I say *namaste* and imagine them showered in light for a brief second. It's a mood-boosting energetic lift each time.

But the practice doesn't have to continue throughout the day; just when you wake up in the morning is sufficient. As I've mentioned, it is most beneficial to do your spiritual exercises before interacting with the rest of the world—that's how you start training the monkey mind. Break the conditioned phone traps. Before you start perusing social media or communicating via text, e-mail, or phone, take a pause. Take a few deep belly breaths and center yourself.

Think about everyone you know you will see today—whether they are people you plan to see, the coffee barista, your family or coworkers, strangers you'll pass on the street, and anyone else you might not know is coming into your life—and send them namaste energy from your heart center. Include those who are responsible for your food and clean water—the farm workers who pick your produce, the garbage collectors, and folks in the service industry.

I recommend you try different methods to see what feels most authentic. Sometimes I picture myself sending love out from my heart that emanates as a light. Or I envision bowing with my hands in a prayer position to those I think about. I even like to picture sprinkling a bit of glittery fairy dust on the people I want to honor. Whatever the way, I imagine a physical representation of sending people love from my heart to theirs. What feels good for you?

I realize this all might seem overwhelming. Keep in mind that for me it takes less than five minutes. As always, your intention is the most important thing of all. You don't need to think about every single person specifically. The idea is to bless and send love to those you will come into contact with today in some way and elevate their frequency with your loving attention.

Sometimes I like to burn a little sacred smoke, too. Eucalyptus is the ideal plant ally for this ritual but, as always, use any herb you feel called to.

GRATITUDE

Remember to take a moment in appreciation, always. You might want to thank yourself for showing up and doing this work, any elements present, and the sacred smoke that supported this practice.

THE LOVERS—TO ALIGN WITH PARTNERSHIP

I really wanted to include a ritual on calling in love, because that's what so many of my clients ask for. But no matter how I wrote it, it just didn't feel authentic. Since authenticity is tantamount to trust, and I want my readers and clients to know with one hundred percent certainty they can always expect me to be real, I am going to share with you the most powerful method I know for opening yourself up to love.

When I launched SMUDGED in 2017, I had a vision of the

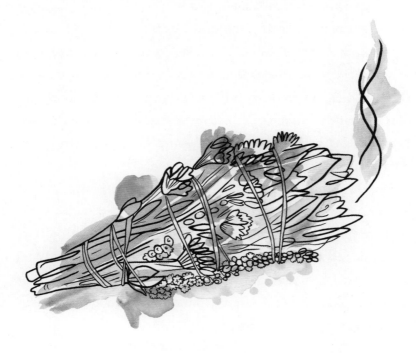

kind of company I wanted to create—the mission, how the products would make people feel, and the ripples of transformation that would take place in our clients' lives through acts of ritual—but the execution was blurry at best. I figured I'd figure it out along the way. So even though I had been working with sacred smoke and making bundles for years, creating something I felt was good enough to sell was a whole other story. Just sourcing wholesale White Sage that was organic, sustainable, ethical, and super high quality was a months-long endeavor.

Finally, I procured the right Sage and it was time to make a prototype. I contacted some artisans who were doing similar work, but none of their samples were quite right. I decided to try making it myself. *No big deal*. I could clearly visualize what I wanted the wand to look like. Still, everything I made fell way short. While still working full time, I made sacred smoke bundles constantly, but none of them met my standards. They looked beautiful and had amazing energy—until they dried, and then, not so much.

I could feel the self-sabotage settling into my bones, so I set a deadline; otherwise I could have easily dragged out the process for years. As the date approached, I was visiting my boyfriend in Miami Beach (I didn't live there yet). My hotel room was covered in flowers, string, and discarded samples. I kept trying to create the vision in my mind's eye, and even though I was close, it just wasn't working.

My man and I had dinner plans and he waited patiently for hours for me to finish so that we could leave. He offered to help and I only said okay because I felt frustrated and was ready to give up. He didn't even ask me details about what I was trying to create and I'm not sure what kind of magic transpired, but we ended up making the wand together, in just a few minutes. He guided me in helping him hold the flowers in the right place as he wrapped the hemp string. Working with someone else got me out of my head and the combination of our efforts resulted in the most gorgeous wand I'd ever seen—it was even more lovely than I'd imagined.

I figured it was only fair that he name it, so I handed him my Kim Krans Wild Unknown tarot deck and asked him to look through the cards and pick the one he felt was most energetically aligned with the wand we just made (he had no knowledge of tarot, but his intuition was on point). My boyfriend chose The Lovers card, and just like that, our first and most popular sacred smoke wand was born.

In the Wild Unknown deck, the card depicts a pair of geese soaring effortlessly in unison and harmony. Their wingspans, necks, and black and white markings are all parallel. The geese are looking straight ahead, not facing each other (as many other decks depict), indicating that while they fit together so naturally as a pair, they also maintain unique and separate identities. While these geese are journeying together, each is also traveling on its own path.

This card, like all tarot cards, has multiple, layered meanings. Its interpretation depends on the deck, the reader, and other cards at play. The overarching significance is obviously about love, one involving a deep bond that goes beyond the flesh—we're talking soul-mate energy. It is also a card that in some decks represents choices about relationships, ones that are not to be made lightly. It carries the energy of ease and flow, and when I look at it I feel calm and hopeful, like everything is exactly as it should be.

You see, so many people are searching for love with such fervor that it aligns with the frequency of worry, fear, and desperation. And no ritual or spell can work while you're vibing on that level. The fact is, if you trust in the divine order of the Universe, you know with certainty that there is no lack—that you are whole and perfect, just as you are. Your heart is then filled with gratitude, hope, and joy. When emanating that kind of signal, with the right timing, you will effortlessly attract a partner.

Said another way: unrequited desire can repel that which you are hoping to attract. If your want is rooted in discontentment, it is intertwined with negative feelings that you're projecting outward about your self-worth, about lack, about feeling desirable. The message you are sending out is one of dissatisfaction, so you are unable to draw love in.

Use our wand, or any sacred herbs, with intention to raise

your frequency and quell your fears. Light it daily and bless yourself, hug yourself, and shower yourself with love. Allow the smoke to waft over you as you make gratitude lists of your blessings, no matter how small—in the morning and before bed, focusing on the best thing that happened that day. Be Pollyanna-like if you have to, full of faith, because with practice you will start feeling different. Make it a choice. Choose your current life and surrender in acceptance of things as they are. Can you be truly happy in this moment? You can decide to be. This is the magic sauce to finding love, success, and everything else that eludes us. When the timing is right, love will reveal itself. Have faith that your partner is looking for you, just as you are searching for them.

In the meantime, let these words by Jalal al-Din Muhammad Rumi, the Persian Sufi mystic, open your heart:

Your task is not
to seek for love,
but merely to
seek and find all
the barriers within yourself
that you have built against it.

I connect with my higher self as a part of my morning practice and before I work with clients, in healing sessions, and when performing reiki or reading tarot cards. In fact, I am unable to read tarot cards accurately without establishing this connection first. There is a clarity that comes through that I don't otherwise have access to. It's almost like I'm looking in on myself. (On the days I do not take the time to foster this relationship, it feels as if I am suffering from brain fog.) The connection will reveal it-self differently for each person, but that sense of clarity almost always comes along.

This particular method was channeled by my healer and teacher Courtney Cooke, who is a graduate of Columbia University's Teachers College, where she studied clinical psychology with a focus on spiritual healing and transformative experiences. She works with the Akashic Records, which are a living source of information that contain the vibrations of a soul's past, present, and foreseeable future. Courtney is not only one of the loveliest people I've ever known, but she is as powerful as she is kind, and this information will be transformational if incorporated into your daily practice.

Courtney says that our higher self is the expression of our spiritual nature, one anchored in love and compassion. When we are willing to learn to connect to our true, nonphysical form, the higher self serves as our internal guidance system, aligning us to our authentic pathway. Whether the trail ahead is familiar or unknown, our higher self knows the most direct, clear, and natural way to proceed.

With awareness and practice, we can learn to sit within the aspect of the higher self at all moments of the day. From this vantage point, we are allowing our hearts to lead as we separate from the ego mind. This ritual connects us again, in another way, to the state of receptivity, revealing our intuition and opening us up to opportunity.

There are many ways to develop and experiment with how to establish a relationship with the higher self. The parts of this exercise from Courtney are in italics, and the rest come from my experience. My suggestion is to start with Courtney's method, practicing it regularly for some time before adding my variances, or your own.

Courtney tells me that she does this practice every morning in meditation and before she meets for healing sessions with her clients. When she is embodying the aspect of the higher self, her decisions and actions are grounded in compassion and have a distinctive clarity. When she is feeling nervous, anxious, or apprehensive about a decision, she calls on her higher self to assist in moving forward.

WHAT YOU'LL NEED

* A chair if you feel called to sit, or you can stand.
* A relic connecting you to an ancestor who has passed—I use the key from my grandmother's jewelry box, as it helps me connect with her energy and guidance.
* Sacred smoke (suggestion: Angelica)
* A piece of paper or journal
* A pen

PERFORM THE RITUAL

1. Open sacred space (page 69).

2. *Sitting in a chair or standing upright, bring your attention to the fourth chakra, the heart space.*

3. Burn a *sacred herb of your choice*, asking the wafting smoke to settle around your heart chakra.

4. With your relic in your hand, ask your ally to help you connect with ease. I say, "Dear Maman, my intention is to connect to my higher self with ease and grace—please help me."

5. *Close your eyes or keep a soft gaze as you shift your awareness from the external to the internal space—feel the subtle energy within the physical body (it could be a warm glow, an opening, or a sense of peace).*

6. *Allow this sensation to linger internally and radiate outward.*

7. *Once the connection has been made, say aloud or silently, "I attune to the frequency of my higher self."*

8. *At this point you may feel a presence arrive at the center of the chest. It may also locate itself in another part of the body or present in a number of varying ways. This is the higher self. Trust it is with you, because it is you.*

9. Take out your paper or journal and ask a question you need some guidance for.

10. Connect to that presence you've just cultivated.

11. Allow your pen to write without thinking or editing. Spend as much time as you have to release the messages coming forth.

12. You can also write a letter from your higher self to someone else's—opening up another layer of communication. I've witnessed this practice completely transform relationships because sometimes it's easier to speak clearly with someone you're having issues with in this way. No communication or mention needs to be made in person.

13. Close sacred space (page 70).

GRATITUDE

Remember to give thanks to Courtney Cooke, the element of Fire, the ancestors and allies you've worked with, your higher self, and that of anyone else you are connecting to.

GLOBAL CHANGE—EMANATING PEACE
AND COMPASSION

Metta meditation, often referred to as loving-kindness meditation, is a practice of projecting peace, kindness, goodwill, and
compassion toward others. The meditation comprises silent, internal repetitions of phrases like *May you be happy* or *May you
feel loved* or *May you be free from suffering*, directed toward a
specific person. It invokes compassion and empathy toward others and opens space to understand another's perspective. This is
my take on *metta*, although I do not call it that. (It's not exactly
the same, and I don't have a specific name for it.)

WHAT YOU'LL NEED

* A quiet, comfortable place where you will be undisturbed
  for the time it takes to complete this process
* Your imagination
* Cleansing room spray, bells, a rattle, or sacred smoke of
  your choice

PERFORM THE RITUAL

1. Set yourself up in a comfortable position for meditation, as
   you will be sitting for a few minutes and want to do your
   best not to fidget.

2. Breathe deeply, inhaling and exhaling through your nose for several rounds.

3. Imagine a light emanating from your heart chakra and surrounding you completely. Any color light that comes into your mind's eye is appropriate. I usually see a pearly iridescent hue. Allow this light to permeate your space and your being. As always, if at any time you have trouble

visualizing, don't worry. Set the intention and trust that you are doing it correctly. The light is shining even if you can't see it.

4. Spread this light further beyond yourself until it's illuminating the whole room—all of your furniture, your walls, windows, plants, and belongings. Take three deep breaths, allowing this light to saturate everything with the vibrations of peace, love, and harmony.

5. Extend the light out further so it sparkles throughout your entire home, inside and outside. See it saturate your pets, the people you share space with, the food in your refrigerator and pantry. Take three deep breaths, allowing the glow to saturate everything with the vibrations of peace, love, and harmony.

6. Next, spread the light emanating from your heart to now include your entire block and all of the homes and businesses therein. Visualize the glow blessing all of your neighbors, the Tree People, the Plant People, the children, and all the little critters who live in your neighborhood. Take three more deep breaths, allowing the iridescent rays to spread with the vibrations of peace, love, and harmony.

7. See this ball of light expand to include your entire state (or that equivalent in your location). Guide it to touch all of the homes, the forests, waters, people, plants, and animals. Ask

the light to elevate the frequency of all that it touches. Take another three breaths here, letting the beams seep into everything with the vibrations of peace, love, and harmony.

8. Now, spread the pearl-colored glow upon your whole country. See it touching all of your countrywomen, sending empathy and compassion to everyone, especially anyone you might be in conflict with. See your heart emanating rays of compassion to those who have opposing political views or who hold foreign opinions, and ask the light to reveal your similarities—reminding yourself that we are much more alike than our egos want us to believe. That in our core, all beings crave the same things—to feel safe and loved. Take three breaths here, allowing the glow to touch the politicians, lawmakers, systems, and communication towers as well.

9. Finally, boomerang your consciousness into space so you are looking down at Earth and yourself shining bright, surrounded by a heavenly glow from somewhere in the Universe. Again, there is no need to make a huge effort here. If you can't see it in your imagination, just speak it and your word will be enough. See your light enveloping the entire planet—blessing Pachamama, the oceans, the dolphins and whales, and every person, animal, plant, flower, and being that exists. Radiate peace, love, and kindness to all of these beings. Take a few deep breaths.

10. Put your hands in prayer at your heart space and whisper:

Dear Universe,

Please show us all a clear path to walk today. One that serves our best and our highest good and that of the world as well. Send all of the angels and allies we need to help us walk this path with grace, ease, and flow.

May we be blessed today. May our hearts and our minds be filled with peace. May we feel safe and loved.

Aho. Amen. And so it shall be!

11. Use a cleaning spray, ring bells, shake a rattle, or burn sacred smoke to clear any negativity you might have picked up from connecting to so many.

GRATITUDE

As always, connecting to the energy of gratitude is the best way to finish a ritual. Please take a moment to cultivate appreciation for the elements, allies, and tools that showed up in support of this beautiful practice.

Magic occurs when we use energy with conscious intent and awareness to attain a better understanding of the world and harmonize with it.

INTEGRATION

Thank you for trusting me to guide you through the rituals that have transformed my life. I hope you know by now that I practice them almost daily. Everything I've shared has been an integral part of my journey to where I am at this very moment. Integration is the act of taking the knowledge you've accumulated and incorporating it into your regular life. The practices and rituals in this book are not meant to be done just once and then forgotten. A real commitment to living on a spiritual path is necessary to see authentic and permanent shifts for the better.

This isn't to say you have to strive to become a monk. Think about it in terms of feng shui. If you try to redecorate your home, incorporating all of the principles of feng shui in one month, you will probably feel confused, overwhelmed, and give up the whole endeavor because those kinds of drastic changes are too intense to introduce all at once. Choosing one or two areas of change will be more manageable and provide a foundation for you to do more when you feel ready.

So how can you incorporate these rituals into the everyday? First of all, don't go ham. Fill out the chart in chapter one (page 22) and decide what area of life you would like to work on first. Start somewhere that doesn't feel overwhelming. Then set a clear, singular intention. Make a forty-day commitment—go all in. At the end of those forty days, assess how you are feeling, and what has changed or remained the same.

Revisit the chart in chapter one and add another layer of ritual into your life. Use the New Moon to set intentions and Full Moons to release everything that no longer serves you (page 56). Burn something often, and make it a subconscious habit to give gratitude to your ancestors and connect to them. Ask what guidance they have to bestow upon you. If you are willing to listen and be patient, the answers will come.

Without integrating these processes in a doable way and moving slowly and steadily, there's a good chance you will burn out or be unable to maintain your energy, like a short circuit. I invite you to take advantage of the groups and other offerings the SMUDGED community offers through our website and social media. Participating in group rituals, even virtually, exponentially adds to their power and will help you integrate this important work into your life because you will feel seen and supported.

Sending so much love to you all.

XO,

A NOTE ABOUT PLANT ALLIES

I have always been drawn to flowers (blame it on my name). My name, Neeloufar, means *Water Lily* (everyone calls me Neelou because no one in the Western Hemisphere can pronounce my name correctly). Names carry power. They influence our lives and our characters. As a kid, I spent countless hours talking to and playing among the Plant People who protect us. As an adult, I've always filled my home with flowers. There is medicine and magic in nature, and flora help us harness the boundless energy of Pachamama.

The six plant allies I describe in this section are the ones I burn most often. Each is used for cleansing and protection purposes—that is their one commonality. These Plant People clear our energetic and auric field so that we can become more aligned with nature and our true selves. I recommend working with the herbs, flowers, seeds, and plants you feel called to, steering clear of others; if there is a specific ally that is speaking to your heart, trust that. You will find that you are drawn to certain Plant People over others, and this will change depending on your circumstances. With time, you will develop a subtle knowing as to which energy you need. Start off by experimenting.

Originally, I was going to include an appendix with basic information on all of the medicinal plants I enjoy working with. But since they frequently change, and the purposes of our plant allies are unique to each individual, I decided to catalog only my go-tos. I encourage you to start with the Plant People who are a part of your local landscape, or the ones you feel most drawn to, and see what magic they teach.

ANGELICA (*GOLPAR* IN FARSI)

This is a difficult herb to procure in the United States—but it's not impossible. Angelica has an earthy smell and has a similar coloring to straw. In Iran, we grind this beautiful and pungent seed and place it on pomegranate seeds during the winter months and especially on the winter solstice—Shab-e Yalda. I prefer to use the seeds when they are whole, not ground, as I am more drawn to the smoke in that form. No matter what way you use it, *Golpar* brings in the highest level of protection and purification. I use this plant ally regularly, almost daily, as an energetic gateway to the Angelic Realm that imbues my everyday rituals with magic.

ROSE

Plants each have their own unique frequency, with Rose being one of the highest at around 320 megahertz. I use this fragrant flower in many of our products because she feels like a portal to Divine beauty and self-confidence. Roses and love simply go together. This flower softens your defenses, creating an opening to the energy of unconditional love. This beautiful energy is healing. It brings joy, protection, and peace within our hearts.

Roses promote the spirit of generosity and gratitude. They ignite a confidence boost because they act as a witness to your innate beauty, allowing a glimpse of reality through their rose-tinted lenses. This flower is also fiercely protective when placed in your field. Not only will Rose protect and uplift your space, but she will do the same for anyone you come into contact with.

WILD RUE (*ESFAND* IN FARSI)

This is the herb that my Maman and all of the women in my family use as sacred smoke. I love the smell, even though for most it's an acquired taste. (*Esfand* is quite popular in the Middle East and I refer to it as the third-degree black belt of sacred smoke.) These earthy brown seeds remove blockages, dissipate self-sabotage, transform negativity, and dispel lower vibrational energies and people. Bad juju, begone.

WHITE SAGE

White Sage is trendy for a reason: it's powerful and smells divine when burning. It's native to Southern California, where I grew up. For centuries, this plant ally has been used ceremonially by many Native tribes in North America to encourage psychic detox, to raise one's energy level, and for purification on many levels. I use it to cleanse spaces of subtle (and not so subtle) stale energies in preparation for fresh intentions. White Sage can also cleanse a person's aura of stagnant energies in advance of ceremony or spiritual work. It diminishes any turmoil in your life as you prepare to embark on new ventures with positive vibrations. It is critical, as ever, to live in right relation with the Earth, so if you do want to work with White Sage in particular, please be sure to procure from a sustainable source—or choose a similar herb that is local to you.

PALO SANTO

I'm so fond of Palo Santo, I named my rescue Chihuahua mix after this mystical tree that grows on the coast of South America. Contrary to misinformation passed around on the Internet, this plant ally is not endangered. In fact, SMUDGED Palo Santo is sustainably wild-harvested from Ecuador (or sometimes Peru) from naturally fallen trees and branches—their magic is activated during the four to ten years they lie dead before being harvested—so trees are never cut down for the purposes of procurement. Palo Santo has been used for centuries by the indigenous people of the Andes for purifying, cleansing, and banishing negative energies. I use Palo Santo almost daily—for focus, to inspire creativity, and of course, for cleansing and protection. My most creative clients are drawn to this holy wood and I wouldn't have been able to write this book without it.

This sacred smoke has a gentle citrus aroma with notes of Myrrh and Frankincense. On a more practical level—it also keeps away mosquitoes and other flying insects. Its uplifting scent raises your vibration in preparation for meditation and allows for a deeper connection to Spirit. It is said that Palo Santo enhances creativity and brings good fortune to those who are open to its magic. It is traditionally used for relieving common colds, flu symptoms, stress, asthma, headaches, anxiety, depression, inflammation, and emotional pain. If I had to pick only one plant ally to burn, it would be this.

LAVENDER

Lavender has been used for centuries to promote calm, healing, protection, and love. As I've mentioned, we use this herb in many of our products. You can grow Lavender in much of the North American continent (and around the world), so try growing some in your home or garden. I personally use it regularly for restorative purposes. Magically, Lavender invites peace of heart and peace of mind by resolving subconscious doubts and fears. It also dissipates conflicts and aids in decision making. Use it in baths to reduce stress and anxiety. In dryer sachets and teas to boost your mood. And as sacred smoke before rituals to welcome your ancestors and allies from other realms, or during meditation for a deeper connection to Spirit.

GRATITUDE

My Grandmothers, I am so grateful for all of the love you showed me while you were here. You were the best part of my child-hood and I cherish the memories I have of both of you. I will always hold you close to my heart and I wish we had more time together. There is so much of my life I want to share with you and while I miss you, *so* much, I can still feel your presence guiding me. I hope you stay close to me, forevermore.

Mom and Dad, I want to express how tremendously grateful I am for you both. I've gotten to spend a lot of time with you this past year and the pandemic has brought us closer together. I can't imagine it was easy to raise a kid whose experience of the world was so different than yours but even though sometimes I was oblivious to it, you have been loving and supportive throughout my life. I so appreciate that. I love you.

My family and close friends, a huge thank-you for all of your time, energy, and effort in this whole process—all of the passes you read, the cover art you considered, the late-night phone calls you answered, and all of the ways in which you have supported me during this time. Thank you for believing in me, always, especially when self-doubt crept in. With grace and little judgment, you've put up with my many moods and the stress that comes with being an entrepreneur. I see you.

Louise Androlia, my redheaded witch sister and illustrator. I feel certain we have spent many lifetimes together and I'm so grateful for your heart and your remarkable talent. This book could not have come to life without you. I remember the hours we spent together on the phone processing life, art, community, society, and everything else—you gave me perspective when the world felt like chaos. I cannot wait to see what we create together next.

Thank you to Katherine Latshaw, my fierce, kind, and tireless literary agent. You helped me when I was running on fumes and I'm not sure I would have made it through the editing process if it weren't for you. I adore, admire, and respect you.

This book is the creation of an incredible team of women at TarcherPerigee—thank you all! I'm especially grateful to my amazing editor, Nina Shield, whose insights were invaluable. Your notes allowed me to write more authentically, revealing who I naturally am. Thank you for believing in the value of these rituals and for trusting in me.

Maryam Rumi, my talented, beautiful designer. I'm so grateful for your connection to Spirit and your ability to understand my creative direction seemingly through osmosis. You breathe life and high vibrations into everything you've created for SMUDGED.

Courtney Cooke, my modern-day oracle. You are an angelic presence in my life. Your work has supported me mentally, physically, and spiritually and this book exists because of your guidance.

Marianne Williamson, thank you for being a mentor and for teaching me how to transmute chaos into clarity. Your interpretations of *A Course In Miracles* have had a profound impact on my interpersonal relationships and my path in this life.

Hunter Becerra, I am forever grateful for your help with SMUDGED during those first couple of years. You were not only instrumental in creating our first sacred smoke wand, but your lighthearted energy balanced mine. Thank you for continuing to teach me how to love unconditionally.

José and Lena Stevens, founders of The Power Path, your teachings have changed the way I view *everything* and have shaped the foundation for how I spend my time here on Earth. I am eternally grateful for your community and the knowledge and traditions you continue to share.

I hold the lineages who have contributed to rituals in this book in sacred reverence. Not only my own ancestral Persian lineage and the ancient Zoroastrian religion, but also the Shipibo people of Peru, the Hindu religion, the Huichol of Mexico, and all of the other religions, indigenous cultures, and communities who share a collective experience with sacred smoke rituals. I am so grateful for your teachings and the medicine you have shared.

Thank you, Pachamama, for giving us all that we need to thrive in this life. I'm grateful to the Sun, Moon, the stars, and all of the elements, especially Fire, for facilitating deep transformation. And *deep* gratitude, from my heart, for all of the animals, angels, allies, herbs, flowers, plants, and tools that come together to create a container of support for magic.

And for everyone who reads this book, I'm so grateful for every single one of you. I'm thankful for every product you've purchased, workshop you've attended, all of the follows, likes, and shares given. Thank you for all of the ways you support SMUDGED and myself. It's because of you that I show up, even when I don't feel like it. Your energy nourishes me and gives me purpose and the inspiration to share my work with the world even when it feels challenging.

My prayer for anyone who picks up this book, this collective of beautiful souls, is peace of heart and peace of mind. May the rituals in this book rain blessings on every facet of your lives. May they enrich your world with beauty, love, abundance, and laughter. May you be surrounded with kind, supportive, open-hearted people who embrace you, wish the best for you, and support your leveling up. I love you. Thank you.

ABOUT THE AUTHOR AND ILLUSTRATOR

Neelou Malekpour was born in Seattle and raised in Tehran, Iran, before moving to Los Angeles at the time of the Iranian revolution. She started SMUDGED as a tribute to her late grandmother, who was her best friend, and who taught her about smudging and how to be responsible for the vibration she put out into the world.

Neelou attended the University of Southern California, where she received a BA in English literature with an emphasis in creative writing and a JD from St. John's University School of Law. She worked on a pilot peacekeeping initiative in the Department of Peacekeeping Operations at the United Nations before becoming a consultant. She has worked with brands such as UNICEF, YogaWorks, 1 Hotels, Selina, Soho House, Sydell Group, Guerilla Union, Real Dog Rescue, and more.

In 2017, she founded SMUDGED, which helps clients attain, and maintain, an elevated frequency through intentional acts of daily ritual, using natural products. Neelou is committed to mindful and ethical business practices; everything she creates is handmade in Miami Beach or Los Angeles, and SMUDGED donates eleven percent of all proceeds to charity.

As a writer, she has contributed to publications such as *Metro NY*, the *Los Angeles Daily News*, *US Weekly*, *Harper's Bazaar*, and more. In 2016, she produced the award-winning film *Guys Reading Poems*.

She currently lives between Miami Beach and Los Angeles with her rescue pup, Palo Santo, and dreams of moving to France. Her favorite color is kelly green and she loves the scent of night.

Louise Androlia is a British fine artist and illustrator. Classically trained in Florence, Italy, and at the Chelsea College of Art in London, she currently resides in Los Angeles. Her work has been featured in numerous international publications, including *Vogue*, *The Sunday Times*, *The Guardian*, and *Rookie* magazine.

Her fine art work is held in private collections in London, Los Angeles, and New York City. Her current work focuses on exploring her neurodivergence via introspective nudes, painted photographs, and narrated watercolor sketches.

Special interests include her cat, Princess Kitty Tiger Pants, birdwatching, astrology, human psychology, three-hour baths, and one hundred percent cacao.

We are shown through the alchemy of smoke and fire that the practice of smudging is one of reverence for the moment. That it holds space for the safety and sanctity of Divine connection. Smudging can bring an important view—one that tells us to look intently, so that we can see reflected the miracle of our own being and its capacity for constant renewal. As in, just as flame ignites substance and creates from this exchange an entirely different manifestation, so too are we able to be scorched and cleansed. Made new for the healing of those around us.

—Liza Fenster

The author will donate a portion of her proceeds
from *The Art of Sacred Smoke* to the charitable organization
the Center for Shamanic Education and Exchange, with a focus on
honoring and sustaining the Shipibo and the Huichol.

TarcherPerigee
an imprint of Penguin Random House LLC
penguinrandomhouse.com

Grateful acknowledgment is made for permission to reprint from the following:
Jenn Campus, Lori Bregman, and Liza Fenster. Text reprinted with permission of the authors.
"Conflict Resolution for Holy Beings" from *Conflict Resolution for Holy Beings: Poems* by Joy Harjo.
Copyright © 2015 by Joy Harjo. Used by permission of W. W. Norton & Company. *Change Me Prayers*
by Tosha Silver. Copyright © 2015 Tosha Silver. Reprinted with permission of Atria Books, a division
of Simon & Schuster. All rights reserved. "What Does 'Namaste' Actually Mean?" by Isabelle Marsh.
Reprinted with permission of MindBodyGreen.com.

Most TarcherPerigee books are available at special quantity discounts for bulk purchase for sales
promotions, premiums, fund-raising, and educational needs. Special books or book excerpts also can
be created to fit specific needs. For details, write: SpecialMarkets@penguinrandomhouse.com.

Library of Congress Cataloging-in-Publication Data

Names: Malekpour, Neelou, author.
Title: The art of sacred smoke: energy-balancing rituals to
cleanse, protect, and empower / Neelou Malekpour.
Description: [New York]: TarcherPerigee, an imprint of
Penguin Random House LLC, [2021] | Includes index. |
Identifiers: LCCN 2021017332 (print) | LCCN 2021017333 (ebook) |
ISBN 9780593329450 (hardcover) | ISBN 9780593329467 (ebook)
Subjects: LCSH: Smoke—Miscellanea. | Plants—Miscellanea. |
Self-care, Health—Miscellanea. | Spiritual healing and spiritualism.
Classification: LCC BF1623.I52 M35 2021 (print) |
LCC BF1623.I52 (ebook) | DDC 133.4/4—dc23
LC record available at https://lccn.loc.gov/2021017332
LC ebook record available at https://lccn.loc.gov/2021017333

Printed in China
10 9 8 7 6 5 4 3 2 1

Book design by Katy Riegel

Illustrations by Louise Androlia